Empowered

THE AMAZING CHURCH OF JESUS CHRIST

From the team who brought you *The Amazing Collection: The Bible, Book by Book*

BIG DREAM
MINISTRIES

ISBN 10: 1-932199-87-1
ISBN 13: 978-1932-199-87-1

Cover design by Useful Group
Cover photo from iStock
Creative Team: Leslie Strader, Patricia Arps, Terry Behimer, Pat Harley, Traci Martin,
    Patricia Reinheimer, and Fay Runnion

Maps from the Holman Bible Atlas © 1998
B&H Publishing Group
Used with permission

Printed in the United States

1 2 3 4 5 6 7 8 9 10 / 25 24 23 22 21 20

Table of Contents

Introduction to Study

By Traci Martin

Jesus prepared His disciples for three years during His earthly ministry. His final command was to go into Judea, Samaria, and the ends of the world to preach the gospel. The Gospel—the good news that Jesus made the ultimate sacrifice for those who would believe. People were coming to saving faith by the thousands. One Jewish man, Saul of Tarsus, burned with passion against the new Christians and persecuted them fully. That is until Jesus appeared before him. Now, the greatest persecutor of Christians became the greatest evangelist of all time—spreading the good news of Christ around the known world.

Through the power of the Holy Spirit, lives were changed, and the body of Christ grew—as The Amazing Church.

Until Christ returns again, we are to continue to build His bride—the Church. Continue Acts 1:8.

Our prayer for you as you study the book of Acts, is that you see the power of the Holy Spirit to transform lives to be used by Christ. He has a plan for you in His Kingdom.

ABOUT THIS STUDY

THEME:
This twelve-week study takes an intimate look into the new but familiar work of the Holy Spirit as He initiates and directs the growth of the Church and the spread of the Gospel through the triumphs and sufferings of Christ's faithful witnesses. The Holy Spirit is the hope of "something greater" that Jesus repeatedly promised, and His arrival in the book of Acts makes clear that there is a purpose beyond the here and now that they — and we — have been called and prepared to fulfill.

TEACHING:
Weekly teaching will offer additional instruction that will enhance understanding of the work of the Spirit in the spread of the Gospel message. Each section of Scripture will unfold in a way that will draw your heart into the story and help you experience the great impact God's people and their message of hope had on the world through the power of the Holy Spirit.

INTRODUCTION:
To help calibrate the timeline and set your mind, take time to read through the introduction at the beginning of each week. This will give you an overview of what you will be studying and orient you as we journey with the Gospel and its messengers where the Holy Spirit led.

MAPS:
Where relevant to the content of the passage, maps are included to give an additional visual connection and understanding about the land and sea travels of those called to spread the Gospel "to the ends of the earth."

MEMORY VERSES:
Each week begins with a verse from the passage of Scripture you'll be studying. Ask the Holy Spirit to help you commit these short verses to memory, and you will be encouraged by the truths written on your heart for the rest of your life!

SCRIPTURE:
We have included the portions of Acts that you will be studying each day in the workbook itself. Have your Bible or Bible app close by so that you can look up additional cross-references throughout the study. Having the passage right in front of you will help with continuity and focus. Context matters, so open your Bible at any point along the way to get a bigger picture of the scene.

QUESTIONS:
Each week of *Empowered: The Amazing Church of Jesus Christ* is divided into five studies rather than five days. Each section contains an introduction and questions about the passage that draw on the Bible study methods of observation, interpretation, and application.

- Before you begin your study each day, pray that the Holy Spirit would illuminate the truths of Scripture to you. Pray that you would grow in your love for Jesus and for the lost around you. Ask the Lord to give you a Spirit-fueled boldness for every circumstance, like Peter and Paul, and eyes to see opportunities to share your faith.
- Read completely through the blocked passage of Scripture before answering the questions.
- To encourage personal study, many questions are about the passage itself and will direct you to prayerfully think and observe truths from God's Word. The application questions will help you apply the truths of the passage to your own life.
- For days you have less time for homework, the questions marked with the ☼ are for **A Quick Study**. These questions focus only on the essentials as you move through the passage. Perfect for keeping pace with your Bible study group during the busy seasons of life.
- Sometimes, you'll discover a section titled **A Deeper Look**. This portion is optional but will lead you into a deeper investigation of a specific truth seen in God's Word.

About This Study

THE BOOK OF ACTS

BEFORE YOU BEGIN

Conservative scholars believe the most likely date for Acts to have been written was circa 62 A.D., after the book of Mark was written and probably before the death of Paul.

The content in the book of Acts spans about thirty years. This is not a complete history of the Church but does build the bridge of transition from the Old to New Covenant (and Testaments) after the death and resurrection of Jesus, the Messiah.

Acts shines a spotlight on the work of the Holy Spirit like no other book in the Bible. In Acts, we will see the Spirit powerfully work through God's people as the foundation of the Church is laid and the message of the Gospel is spread. We will read accounts of many men and women who were used in miraculous ways to carry out the Great Commission. But, as with the entirety of Scripture, each story should cause us to give praise to the triune God, who is seen as never before in these twenty-eight chapters. Ask Him to give you eyes to see the glorious work of the Father, Son, and Holy Spirit each time you open His Word.

WEEK 1 TEACHING NOTES

Map of Early Church Expansion

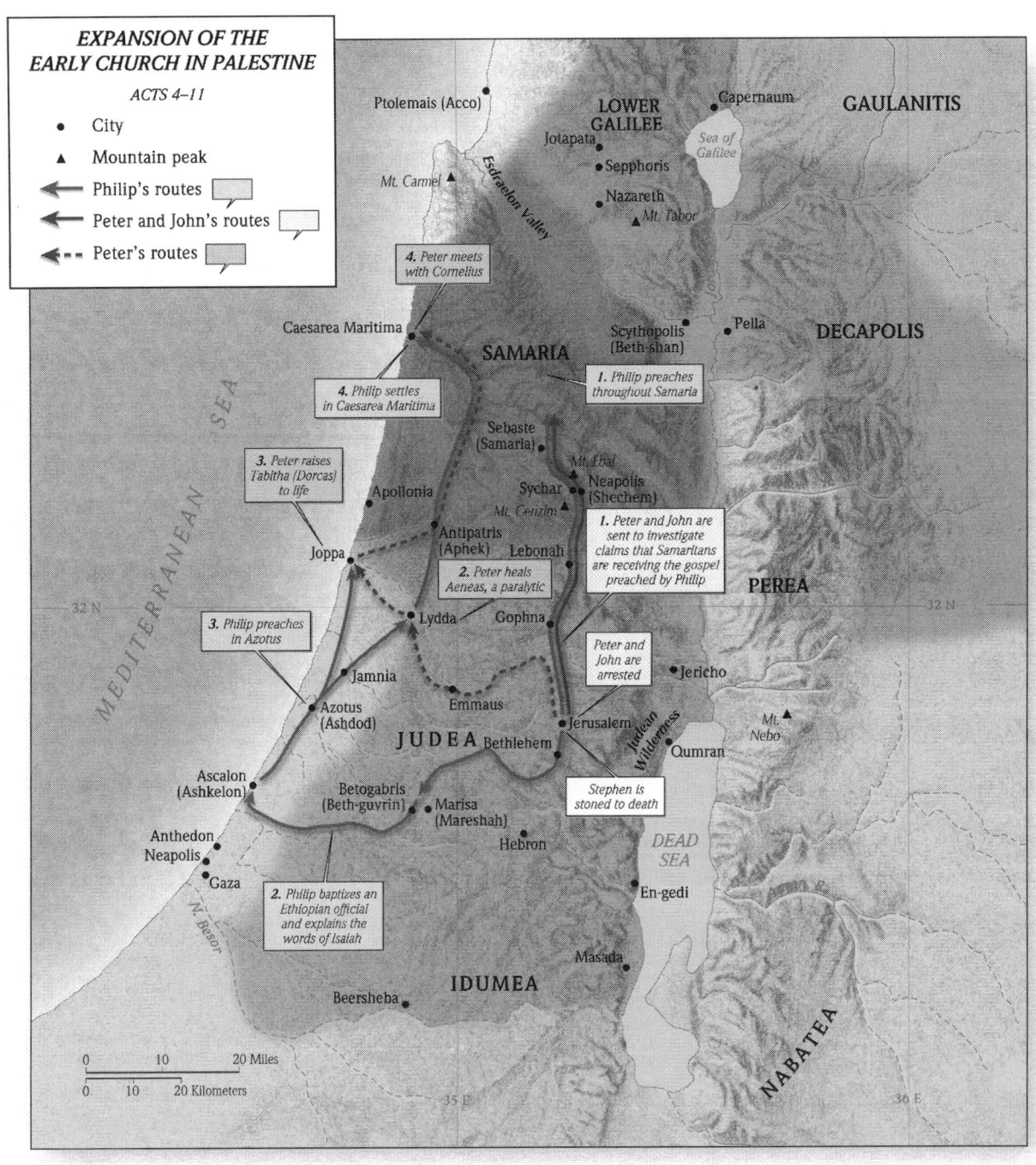

EXPANSION OF THE EARLY CHURCH IN PALESTINE

ACTS 4–11

- • City
- ▲ Mountain peak
- ← Philip's routes
- ← Peter and John's routes
- ◄- - Peter's routes

4. Peter meets with Cornelius

4. Philip settles in Caesarea Maritima

1. Philip preaches throughout Samaria

3. Peter raises Tabitha (Dorcas) to life

1. Peter and John are sent to investigate claims that Samaritans are receiving the gospel preached by Philip

2. Peter heals Aeneas, a paralytic

3. Philip preaches in Azotus

Peter and John are arrested

Stephen is stoned to death

2. Philip baptizes an Ethiopian official and explains the words of Isaiah

Ptolemais (Acco)

LOWER GALILEE

Capernaum

GAULANITIS

Jotapata

Sea of Galilee

Sepphoris

Mt. Carmel ▲

Esdraelon Valley

Nazareth

▲ Mt. Tabor

Caesarea Maritima

SAMARIA

Scythopolis (Beth-shan)

Pella

DECAPOLIS

Sebaste (Samaria)

Mt. Ebal ▲

Neapolis (Shechem)

Sychar

Mt. Gerizim ▲

Apollonia

MEDITERRANEAN SEA

Antipatris (Aphek)

Lebonah

PEREA

Joppa

32 N

Lydda

Gophna

32 N

Jamnia

Emmaus

Jericho

Azotus (Ashdod)

JUDEA

Bethlehem

Jerusalem

Judean Wilderness

Mt. Nebo ▲

Qumran

Ascalon (Ashkelon)

Betogabris (Beth-guvrin)

Marisa (Mareshah)

Hebron

DEAD SEA

Anthedon Neapolis

En-gedi

Gaza

N. Besor

Masada

Beersheba

IDUMEA

NABATEA

| 0 | 10 | 20 Miles |
| 0 | 10 | 20 Kilometers |

35 E

36 E

Empowered: The Amazing Church of Jesus Christ

Acts 1–2

The Early Church in Jerusalem

The book of Acts begins with an ending. After a familiar introduction from Luke—a Gospel writer, Gentile physician, and leader in the early Church—we see the final scene of the Gospels continued here, with Jesus ascending to His Father's right hand (Romans 8:34). The resurrected Jesus had been "appearing and speaking" to His followers for more than a month. And even though they'd just witnessed the greatest miracle of all, the disciples were still looking for an immediate, earthly kingdom.

The kingdom of God on earth is inaugurated in Acts, and Luke shows it is connected to the coming of the Holy Spirit. At first, the Holy Spirit was just an idea to these men and women—the hope that Jesus repeatedly promised would provide all they needed, the Helper who would come to fill, teach, and guide (John 14:26, 16:13). His arrival during the Feast of Weeks made it clear there was a purpose, beyond what their eyes could see, that they had been called and empowered to fulfill.

Before a throng of curious and attentive Jews from across the known world, a Spirit-filled Peter preached the sermon of his life, and thousands were led to Christ by faith. This was not only the beginning of a mission to save souls, it was the dawn of the Church—men and women gathering to encourage, give, sacrifice, and worship, with truth on their minds and eternity in their hearts.

KEY VERSE

"But you will receive power when the Holy Spirit has come on you; and you shall be my witnesses both in Jerusalem, and in all Judea and Samaria, and even to the remotest part of the earth."

ACTS 1:8

STUDY ONE | Acts 1:1–14 | Wait for the Promise

Luke opens his letter to Theophilus (which means "lover of God") with a summary of the forty days after Jesus' resurrection, an assurance of hope, and a commission that compels us still today. At their final meeting, the disciples' expectations of earthly glory were quickly and firmly redirected by Jesus who, instead of knowledge, promised power greater than anything they could imagine. As Jesus' earthly ministry came to an end, the ministry of these newly ordained missionaries began. And His glorious departure was a pre-view of His second coming—the day heaven will open for those who are alive in Christ to be caught up "in the clouds to meet the Lord in the air" (1 Thessalonians 4:17). In the meantime, the disciples were to go and bear witness to the abundant life Jesus offers now and forever to all who call on His name.

---

1 The first account I composed, Theophilus, about all that Jesus began to do and teach, **2** until the day when He was taken up to heaven, after He had by the Holy Spirit given orders to the apostles whom He had chosen. **3** To these He also presented Himself alive after His suffering, by many convincing proofs, appearing to them over a period of forty days and speaking of the things concerning the kingdom of God. **4** Gathering them together, He commanded them not to leave Jerusalem, but to wait for what the Father had promised, "Which," He said, "you heard of from Me; **5** for John baptized with water, but you will be baptized with the Holy Spirit not many days from now."

6 So when they had come together, they were asking Him, saying, "Lord, is it at this time You are restoring the kingdom to Israel?" **7** He said to them, "It is not for you to know times or epochs which the Father has fixed by His own authority; **8** but you will receive power when the Holy Spirit has come upon you; and you shall be My witnesses both in Jerusalem, and in all Judea and Samaria, and even to the remotest part of the earth."

9 And after He had said these things, He was lifted up while they were look-ing on, and a cloud received Him out of their sight. **10** And as they were gazing intently into the sky while He was going, behold, two men in white clothing stood beside them. **11** They also said, "Men of Galilee, why do you stand looking into the sky? This Jesus, who has been taken up from you into heaven, will come in just the same way as you have watched Him go into heaven."

12 Then they returned to Jerusalem from the mount called Olivet, which is near Jerusalem, a Sabbath day's journey away. **13** When they had entered the city, they went up to the upper room where they were staying; that is, Peter and John and James and Andrew, Philip and Thomas, Bartholomew and Matthew, James the son of Alphaeus, and Simon the Zealot, and Judas the son of James. **14** These all with one mind were continually devoting themselves to prayer, along with the women, and Mary the mother of Jesus, and with His brothers.

---

1. Luke tells us that Jesus provided not just one or two but "many convincing proofs" to His followers that He was truly alive after His suffering and death on the cross. Read the verses below. What were some of the convincing proofs of Jesus' resurrection?

   Matthew 28:9

   Mark 16:9–12

Empowered: The Amazing Church of Jesus Christ

Luke 24:36−43

John 21:1

1 Corinthians 15:5−7

 2. What was Jesus' two-fold command in Acts 1:4? Who is it that the Father had promised in verse 5?

How did this confirm what was foretold in Luke 3:15−16?

 3. What did Jesus say would happen next in Acts 1:8? (note the order of events) What did Jesus say the Holy Spirit would accomplish?

4. Jesus mentions Acts 1:8 in His commission to the disciples. Review the map on page 12 and note where each region is located. Then read the brief descriptions of each location.

Jerusalem: This was the most important city in the Bible and the center of religious life for the Jews. In many ways, this was comfortable and familiar territory for the disciples.

Judea: The southern portion of Israel and represents the ancient kingdom of Judah. At this time, Judea was a Roman province surrounding Jerusalem that was predominantly Jewish.

Samaria: Samaria refers to the northern portion of Israel and represents the ancient kingdom of Israel. It was inhabited by Samaritans, a half-Jew, half-Gentile race that came about after the Assyrian captivity of the northern kingdom of Israel when Jews intermarried with their Assyrian captors (circa 721 B.C.). The Samaritans had their own Temple, their own copy of the Torah, and had no dealings at all with the Jews. (John 4:9)

What would be some of the benefits of being witnesses here? What would be some of the challenges?

5. As this earthly scene closes, a heavenly one begins. Read Ephesians 1:20–21 and record what you learn about Jesus' return to heaven, His reception, and His role.

6. The "cloud" Luke describes in Acts 1:9 is not the same kind of cumulus or stratus we see when we look skyward. There are several references to a particular kind of cloud throughout Scripture. Look up ONE of the following verses and record what you learn.

Exodus 16:10   Daniel 7:13
Exodus 19:9   Revelation 14:14
Numbers 9:15–23

7. Describe the scene in the upper room in Acts 1:13–14. Who was there? What were the followers of Jesus doing while they "wait(ed) for what the Father had promised?" (Acts 1:4)

STUDY TWO | Acts 1:15–26
Appointing the Twelfth Apostle

The disciples found some closure to their "old" life as their leader, Peter, walked them through a biblical understanding of Judas' betrayal and a prayerful decision to replace him. Truth comforts and instructs in this scene, as the sovereignty of God worked through the hands of these chosen men. It was a high calling to follow in the footsteps of Jesus, and the one designated to be a witness along with the eleven others must have been taught and shepherded by Jesus Himself. A close connection to Christ sheds light on sin and assures a faith refined. These would be invaluable gifts to these chosen ministers in the days and years to come.

---

15 At this time Peter stood up in the midst of the brethren (a gathering of about one hundred and twenty persons was there together), and said, **16** "Brethren, the Scripture had to be fulfilled, which the Holy Spirit foretold by the mouth of David concerning Judas, who became a guide to those who arrested Jesus. **17** For he was counted among us and received his share in this ministry." **18** (Now this man acquired a field with the price of his wickedness, and falling headlong, he burst open in the middle and all his intestines gushed out. **19** And it became known to all who were living in Jerusalem; so that in their own language that field was called Hakeldama, that is, Field of Blood.) **20** "For it is written in the book of Psalms,

'Let his homestead be made desolate,
And let no one dwell in it';
and,
'Let another man take his office.'

21 Therefore it is necessary that of the men who have accompanied us all the time that the Lord Jesus went in and out among us— **22** beginning with the baptism of John until the day that He was taken up from us—one of these must become a witness with us of His resurrection." **23** So they put forward two men, Joseph called Barsabbas (who was also called Justus), and Matthias. **24** And they prayed and said, "You, Lord, who know the hearts of all men, show which one of these two You have chosen **25** to occupy this ministry and apostleship from which Judas turned aside to go to his own place." **26** And they drew lots for them, and the lot fell to Matthias; and he was added to the eleven apostles.

1. Describe the scene in verse 15 in your own words. Where were they? Who was there? What do you think His followers were feeling at this time? Explain your answer.

2. Read Luke 24:25 in your Bible. What does this verse tell us about the disciples' grasp of Jesus' purpose during His time on earth?

3. Peter's words in Acts 1:16 represent a major shift in thinking and understanding for the disciples. Peter notes that David prophesied about Judas in Psalm 41:9. How would this biblical explanation of Judas' betrayal help the men deal with the betrayal from among them?

> In his fit of remorse, Judas cast the 30 pieces of silver onto the temple floor and then hanged himself in a remote field. No one found him until his body had decayed, become bloated, fallen from the noose, landed face down, and burst open, and his organs had spilled onto the ground. ... Ancient people considered this gruesome scene the most shameful way to die and an unthinkable way for a body to decay." Dr. Charles Swindoll, *Swindoll's Living Insights: New Testament Commentary on Acts*

4. What do we learn about Judas in Acts 1:16–19 that adds to Matthew's account in Matthew 27:3–10? How does this illustrate the consequence of Satan's power and control in someone's life?

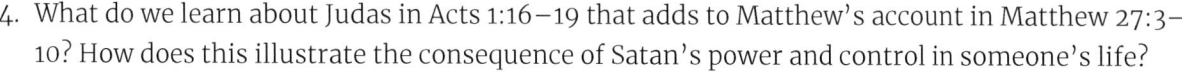

5. What were the requirements for the one who would fill the void left by Judas along with the other apostles? (vv. 21–22) Based on verse 14, what other qualities might have been necessary to fulfill this role?

6. How was the new apostle selected? (vv. 24–26) Who was selected?

7. Read Luke 6:12–16. Who chose the original twelve disciples? Who can we be confident chose this new one?

> "[Casting lots] was a common Old Testament method of determining God's will (Lev. 16:8-10; Joshua 7:14; Prov. 18:18). [Acts 1:26] is the last Biblical mention of lots—the coming of the Spirit [in Acts 2] made them unnecessary." (From John MacArthur Study Bible (ESV).)

STUDY THREE | Acts 2:1–13
The Day of Pentecost

The coming of the Holy Spirit was a sensory experience. The sights and sounds of His arrival were enough to draw a crowd, and this gathering of nations was united not in language, but in understanding. A miracle never seen before or since was taking place: the wonders of God were taught and heard at once in every tongue under heaven. It was surely no accident that Jerusalem—the first stop in the Great Commission—was filled this divinely appointed day with pilgrims who'd come from as far away as the shore of the Mediterranean Sea to the vast Arabian desert and everywhere in between. Here, the first pebble was thrown into the "pond," and its waves almost instantly reached the world.

---

1 When the day of Pentecost had come, they were all together in one place. 2 And suddenly there came from heaven a noise like a violent rushing wind, and it filled the whole house where they were sitting. 3 And there appeared to them tongues as of fire distributing themselves, and they rested on each one of them. 4 And they were all filled with the Holy Spirit and began to speak with other tongues, as the Spirit was giving them utterance.

5 Now there were Jews living in Jerusalem, devout men from every nation under heaven. 6 And when this sound occurred, the crowd came together, and were bewildered because each one of them was hearing them speak in his own language. 7 They were amazed and astonished, saying, "Why, are not all these who are speaking Galileans? 8 And how is it that we each hear them in our own language to which we were born? 9 Parthians and Medes and Elamites, and residents of Mesopotamia, Judea and Cappadocia, Pontus and Asia, 10 Phrygia and Pamphylia, Egypt and the districts of Libya around Cyrene, and visitors from Rome, both Jews and proselytes, 11 Cretans and Arabs—we hear them in our own tongues speaking of the mighty deeds of

God." **12** And they all continued in amazement and great perplexity, saying to one another, "What does this mean?" **13** But others were mocking and saying, "They are full of sweet wine."

---

1. The day of Pentecost is also called the Feast of Weeks or Harvest and is outlined in Deuteronomy 16:9–11. What is the heart attitude that marked this particular event?

2. Describe the coming of the Holy Spirit from the details provided in Acts 2:2–3.

3. The Holy Spirit was given at this moment in history recorded in the New Testament, but His activity is not limited to this period of time. God's Spirit was present even at Creation and has been active throughout history. Read the verses below and underline what you observe about the Spirit's presence and work.

> "Jewish men were required by law to attend the Jewish feast days. These Jewish pilgrims and proselytes came from every nation under heaven. Many of these Jews made an annual pilgrimage back to Jerusalem. Josephus, the Jewish historian who lived at this time, tells us that oftentimes the city of Jerusalem, which normally had a population of 150,000, would be swollen in numbers to well over a million. The city was packed and the suburbs were filled. Pilgrims were camped all along the hillsides." Dr. Jack L. Arnold, sermon on Acts 2, Grace Church, Roanoke, VA

"The earth was formless and void, and darkness was over the surface of the deep, and the Spirit of God was moving over the surface of the waters." Genesis 1:2

"The Spirit of the Lord came upon him (Othniel), and he judged Israel. When he went out to war, the Lord gave Cushan-rishathaim king of Mesopotamia into his hand, so that he prevailed over Cushan-rishathaim." Judges 3:10

"The Spirit of the Lord spoke by me, and His word was on my tongue." 2 Samuel 23:2

"I will put My Spirit within you and cause you to walk in My statutes, and you will be careful to observe My ordinances." Ezekiel 36:27

"The Spirit of the Lord will rest on Him, the spirit of wisdom and understanding, the spirit of counsel and strength, the spirit of knowledge and of the fear of the Lord." Isaiah 11:2

"On the other hand I am filled with power—with the Spirit of the LORD—and with justice and courage to make known to Jacob his rebellious act, even to Israel his sin." Micah 3:8

4. What was the immediate result of the Spirit's indwelling the believers? (Acts 2:4)

5. How did the people who were in Jerusalem at this time respond to the events of verses Acts 2:2–4? (vv. 6–7)

6. Look at the map and circle all the regions mentioned in verses 9–10. What was happening to this diverse group of people at the same time, according to verse 11?

7. What were the two responses to the disciples' proclamation as seen in verses 12–13?

8. The word "filled" or "full" means pervading, diffusing throughout, taking possession of. As believers, we are filled and can be completely controlled by the Holy Spirit, which is the only way we can be conformed into the image of Christ.

Choose at least ONE of the following passages and answer: What are the things that fill us, by His Spirit, as believers?

Romans 5:5   Philippians 1:11
Romans 15:13–14   Colossians 3:16

Choose at least ONE of the following passages and answer: What are the things that Christ followers should not be filled with?

Proverbs 4:23–27   1 Timothy 6:9–10
Colossians 3:5   1 John 2:15–16

9. What are you filled with today—fear, envy, anger, regret? Or have you allowed the Holy Spirit to have full dominion over your heart and mind? What do you need to do to become empty of self and full of Jesus?

A DEEPER LOOK

This section of Acts brings to mind another time where foreign tongues were given in a sudden and purposeful way. God confused man's languages at Babel in Genesis 11:1–9 to scatter mankind around the world, thwarting their self-sufficiency and self-exalting aspirations.

By contrast, the languages or "other tongues" given in Acts 2 are thought of as the reversal of this "curse"—drawing people together by God's Spirit for the purpose of establishing the Church and proclaiming the gospel of Jesus Christ.

On the day of Pentecost, the Lord broke down barriers between nations and people groups and unified hearts by a common faith in the Messiah.

Culture and ethnicity can still divide us today but, one day, "a great multitude... from every nation, from all tribes and peoples and languages" will stand before the throne and worship together (Revelation 7:9, ESV).

What are you doing to understand those who think, act, live, and worship differently from you?

What steps can you take to bring the truth of the gospel to someone who might be hindered by language, culture, or another demographic challenge?

We must put aside our pride, fear, and discomfort to rest in the joy and hope of Psalm 133:1, "How good and how pleasant it is for brothers to dwell together in unity!"

STUDY FOUR | Acts 2:14–36
Peter's First Sermon

A little more than six weeks before this moment in Scripture, Peter, the bold and blustering disciple, betrayed his Lord mere hours after he had sworn to Him that he was ready to count the cost. Restored by the resurrected Jesus on the seashore and now, full of the Holy Spirit, Peter speaks truth to multitudes in a way he never had before. The crowd had questioned, "What does this mean?" and now the words of the prophet Joel and Israel's beloved King David shine light on the One to whom these signs were pointing. Peter—the rock on whom Christ promised to build His Church—was also serving as a shepherd, feeding the sheep out of love for the Savior.

14 But Peter, taking his stand with the eleven, raised his voice and declared to them: "Men of Judea and all you who live in Jerusalem, let this be known to you and give heed to my words. **15** For these men are not drunk, as you suppose, for it is only the third hour of the day; **16** but this is what was spoken of through the prophet Joel:

17 'And it shall be in the last days,' God says,
'That I will pour forth of My Spirit on all mankind;
And your sons and your daughters shall prophesy,
And your young men shall see visions,
And your old men shall dream dreams;
18 Even on My bondslaves, both men and women,
I will in those days pour forth of My Spirit
And they shall prophesy.
19 'And I will grant wonders in the sky above
And signs on the earth below,
Blood, and fire, and vapor of smoke.
20 'The sun will be turned into darkness
And the moon into blood,
Before the great and glorious day of the Lord shall come.
21 'And it shall be that everyone who calls on the name of the Lord will be saved.'
22 "Men of Israel, listen to these words: Jesus the Nazarene, a man attested to you by God with miracles and wonders and signs which God performed through Him in your midst, just as you yourselves know— **23** this Man, delivered over by the predetermined plan and foreknowledge of God, you nailed to a cross by the hands of godless men and put Him to death. **24** But God raised Him up again, putting an end to the agony of death, since it was impossible for Him to be held in its power. **25** For David says of Him,

'I saw the Lord always in my presence;
For He is at my right hand, so that I will not be shaken.
26 'Therefore my heart was glad and my tongue exulted;
Moreover my flesh also will live in hope;
27 Because You will not abandon my soul to Hades,
Nor allow Your Holy One to undergo decay.
28 'You have made known to me the ways of life;
You will make me full of gladness with Your presence.'

29 "Brethren, I may confidently say to you regarding the patriarch David that he both died and was buried, and his tomb is with us to this day. **30** And so, because he was a prophet and knew that God had sworn to him with an oath to seat one of his descendants on his throne, **31** he looked ahead and spoke of the resurrection of the Christ, that He was neither abandoned to Hades, nor did His flesh suffer decay. **32** This Jesus God raised up again, to which we are all witnesses. **33** Therefore having been exalted to the right hand of God, and having received from the Father the promise of the Holy Spirit, He has poured forth this which you both see and hear. **34** For it was not David who ascended

Empowered: The Amazing Church of Jesus Christ

into heaven, but he himself says:

'The Lord said to my Lord,
"Sit at My right hand,
35 Until I make Your enemies a footstool for Your feet."'
    36 Therefore let all the house of Israel know for certain that God has made Him both Lord and Christ—this Jesus whom you crucified."

---

1. Who spoke in verse 14 and what did he ask of his audience?

> One twenty-four-hour period was divided into twelve hours of darkness and twelve hours of daylight, so the third hour of the day would have been 9:00 a.m.

2. In this passage, Peter is operating under the indwelling power of the Holy Spirit for the first time. How is Peter's sermon a fulfillment of Jesus' promises in John 14:25–26?

3. Why would Peter use the Law and Prophets (known to us as the Old Testament) to address their concerns?

4. According to Joel in verses 17–18, who is eligible to receive the Holy Spirit?

   How are the events of Acts 2:1–13 a reflection or illustration of Joel's prophecy?

5. How does Acts 2:21 give you hope and encouragement today? How does it inform your prayers?

6. How does Peter address the sovereignty of God with regard to the crucifixion of Jesus in verses 22–24?

7. How do David's words from Psalm 16 (quoted in vv. 25–28) point to the coming Messiah? What do you notice about David's words that were fulfilled in the death and resurrection of Jesus?

8. How does Peter use David, beloved king of Israel, to establish the true claims of the resurrection? (vv. 29–31)

9. What are the distinct activities of the Trinity seen in verses 32–33?

God the Father:

Jesus the Son:

The Holy Spirit:

STUDY FIVE | Acts 2:37–47
A Spirit of Unity

When we see our sin in the light of God's holiness, the only right response is repentance. The pain the crowd in Jerusalem felt was right and good, and a picture of the kindness of God (Romans 2:4). The Jews who had pierced their Messiah unto death were now pierced themselves, stabbed awake by the over-whelming reality of their desperate need of a Savior. That is a picture of 1 Peter 2:24, "He Himself bore our sins in His body on the cross, so that we might die to sin and live to righteousness; for by His wounds you were healed." After receiving God's gift of forgiveness, grace and gratitude overflowed into the lives of others. And the body of Christ flourished.

---

37 Now when they heard this, they were pierced to the heart, and said to Peter and the rest of the apostles, "Brethren, what shall we do?" **38** Peter said to them, "Repent, and each of you be baptized in the name of Jesus Christ for the forgiveness of your sins; and you will receive the gift of the Holy Spirit.

Empowered: The Amazing Church of Jesus Christ

39 For the promise is for you and your children and for all who are far off, as many as the Lord our God will call to Himself." **40** And with many other words he solemnly testified and kept on exhorting them, saying, "Be saved from this perverse generation!" **41** So then, those who had received his word were baptized; and that day there were added about three thousand souls. **42** They were continually devoting themselves to the apostles' teaching and to fellowship, to the breaking of bread and to prayer.

43 Everyone kept feeling a sense of awe; and many wonders and signs were taking place through the apostles. **44** And all those who had believed were together and had all things in common; **45** and they began selling their property and possessions and were sharing them with all, as anyone might have need. **46** Day by day continuing with one mind in the temple, and breaking bread from house to house, they were taking their meals together with gladness and sincerity of heart, **47** praising God and having favor with all the people. And the Lord was adding to their number day by day those who were being saved.

---

1. How did the crowd respond to Peter's teaching? (v. 37)

2. What are the two questions asked by the crowd in Acts 2:12 and verse 37? How would you respond to someone asking these questions of you about the Gospel?

3. What specific instruction did Peter give in verse 38? What promises are given in verses 38–39?

   How do these verses give you hope and encouragement today?

4. What do verses 40–41 tell us continued to happen and what was the impact on the Church?

5. Read Ephesians 2:1–10. Here we see the miracle of grace that instantly transformed 3,000 hearts that day. What does this look like in your life?

6. Without understanding the context of Acts 2:42–47, we can easily believe the Bible is prescribing communal living. In his Acts commentary, Dr. Dave Guzik explains the reason for what we see in these verses:

"With the influx of more than 3,000 believers, most of whom stayed in Jerusalem and didn't have jobs, the family of Christians had to share if they were to survive. We shouldn't regard this as an early experiment in communism because it was voluntary, temporary, and flawed to the extent that the church in Jerusalem was in continual need of financial support from other churches. Also, we don't have any evidence this continued very long. ... The Jews had a tremendous custom of hospitality during any major feast like Pentecost; all visitors were received into private homes, and no one could charge for giving a bed or a room to a visitor or for supplying their basic needs. The Christians took this tremendous feast-time hospitality and made it an everyday thing." *(www.enduringword.com)*

There are, however, many examples of healthy Christian community seen in these verses that we should strive to follow today. Look at the chart below and compare the ways the Church today still carries out the model of the early Church in Acts 2. Write the letter(s) from the right column in the corresponding blank in the left column (note that some blanks may have multiple letters and some letters will be used more than once).

The Church in Acts 2:42–47	The Church Today
Apostles' teaching _____	A. Open-hearted hospitality (Romans 12:13)
The fellowship _____	B. Devotion to prayer (Colossians 4:2)
Breaking of bread _____	C. Committed community through Bible study or small groups (Hebrews 10:24–25)
Prayer _____	D. Pursing unity (Ephesians 4:1–3)
Together and all things in common _____	E. Remembrance through The Lord's Supper (1 Corinthians 11:23–26)
Selling possessions and distributing to those in need _____	F. Praising God, drawing others in (Romans 15:6–7)
Attending temple together _____	G. Generous response to need (Hebrews 13:16)
Breaking bread in homes _____	H. Consistent preaching/teaching from God's Word (2 Timothy 4:2)
Praising God _____	
Having favor with all people _____	

Empowered: The Amazing Church of Jesus Christ

7. How are verses 42–47 an expression of Acts 1:8?

8. How are you a witness for Christ in the places He sends you today?

9. Are you a member of a local church? Why or why not? What does this passage teach you about the importance of being connected to the body of Christ? Which of these marks of fellowship listed do you experience or participate in regularly? Where do you need to grow?

WEEK 2 TEACHING NOTES

Empowered: The Amazing Church of Jesus Christ

Acts 3–5

Peter and John: Men on a Mission

Bold. Generous. Unified. Growing. These words describe the earliest days of the Church seen in Acts, when persecution was just a possibility and not a way of life. These Spirit-filled believers were strong in their faith and committed to the truth. And the Church was growing by the thousands.

Then, a miraculous healing alerted the religious leaders that the idea of a resurrected Jesus was still alive and well among the people. Peter and John were jailed more than once for their teaching and beliefs but, in the midst of the chaos and persecution, Christ was proclaimed.

When men and women live out the call of Christ, regardless of the circumstances, the results are blessing and glory. But those whose minds are set on the things of the flesh become easy prey for an adversary who revels in darkness. This week, we see what happens not only when we submit to the Spirit's leading, but also how even dabbling in deceit can destroy.

KEY VERSE

"And with great power the apostles were giving testimony to the resurrection of the Lord Jesus, and abundant grace was upon them all."

Acts 4:33

STUDY ONE | Acts 3:1–26
Signs and Wonders in the Temple

Dr. Luke opens this chapter of Acts with the healing of a lame man, a supernatural act that provided another platform for Peter to preach the Gospel. His eager audience was astounded by the medical miracle they observed, so Peter seized the opportunity to pour the balm of spiritual truths on their hurting hearts. Moses, Samuel, Abraham, and the prophets help lay the groundwork for a soul-stirring explanation of the life of Jesus. Sin was pointedly dealt with, but forgiveness generously offered. And the children of Israel were reminded once more of the blessings of their heritage and the place they hold in the heart of God.

---

¹ Now Peter and John were going up to the temple at the ninth hour, the hour of prayer. ² And a man who had been lame from his mother's womb was being

carried along, whom they used to set down every day at the gate of the temple which is called Beautiful, in order to beg alms of those who were entering the temple. **3** When he saw Peter and John about to go into the temple, he began asking to receive alms. **4** But Peter, along with John, fixed his gaze on him and said, "Look at us!" **5** And he began to give them his attention, expecting to receive something from them. **6** But Peter said, "I do not possess silver and gold, but what I do have I give to you: In the name of Jesus Christ the Nazarene—walk!" **7** And seizing him by the right hand, he raised him up; and immediately his feet and his ankles were strengthened. **8** With a leap he stood upright and began to walk; and he entered the temple with them, walking and leaping and praising God. **9** And all the people saw him walking and praising God; **10** and they were taking note of him as being the one who used to sit at the Beautiful Gate of the temple to beg alms, and they were filled with wonder and amazement at what had happened to him.

11 While he was clinging to Peter and John, all the people ran together to them at the so-called portico of Solomon, full of amazement. **12** But when Peter saw this, he replied to the people, "Men of Israel, why are you amazed at this, or why do you gaze at us, as if by our own power or piety we had made him walk? **13** The God of Abraham, Isaac and Jacob, the God of our fathers, has glorified His servant Jesus, the one whom you delivered and disowned in the presence of Pilate, when he had decided to release Him. **14** But you disowned the Holy and Righteous One and asked for a murderer to be granted to you, **15** but put to death the Prince of life, the one whom God raised from the dead, a fact to which we are witnesses. **16** And on the basis of faith in His name, it is the name of Jesus which has strengthened this man whom you see and know; and the faith which comes through Him has given him this perfect health in the presence of you all.

17 "And now, brethren, I know that you acted in ignorance, just as your rulers did also. **18** But the things which God announced beforehand by the mouth of all the prophets, that His Christ would suffer, He has thus fulfilled. **19** Therefore repent and return, so that your sins may be wiped away, in order that times of refreshing may come from the presence of the Lord; **20** and that He may send Jesus, the Christ appointed for you, **21** whom heaven must receive until the period of restoration of all things about which God spoke by the mouth of His holy prophets from ancient time. **22** Moses said, 'THE LORD GOD WILL RAISE UP FOR YOU A PROPHET LIKE ME FROM YOUR BRETHREN; TO HIM YOU SHALL GIVE HEED to everything He says to you. **23** And it will be that every soul that does not heed that prophet shall be utterly destroyed from among the people.' **24** And likewise, all the prophets who have spoken, from Samuel and his successors onward, also announced these days. **25** It is you who are the sons of the prophets and of the covenant which God made with your fathers, saying to Abraham, 'AND IN YOUR SEED ALL THE FAMILIES OF THE EARTH SHALL BE BLESSED.' **26** For you first, God raised up His Servant and sent Him to bless you by turning every one of you from your wicked ways."

Empowered: The Amazing Church of Jesus Christ

1. Several main characters appear in verses 1−2 that will be part of our study all week. Answer "who, what, when, where, and why" that you can observe from these verses.

2. The words "saw," "fixed his gaze," "look," and "give attention" are used in verses 3-5. Based on what we know about this scene so far, why might the idea of seeing be emphasized here?

> For devout Jews, the 9th hour of the day is 3 p.m., one of three Jewish times of prayer. The other time is 9 a.m. (3rd hour) and an evening prayer (See Daniel 6:10 and Psalm 55:17). Scholars believe Peter and John were "Jews being Jewish" and continuing their disciplined practice of prayer. Today, believers are exhorted to "pray without ceasing" (1 Thessalonians 5:17).

3. What did the lame beggar ask for and what did he receive? How would that gift impact his life? (vv.6−8)

4. What happened in Acts 3:7−8 after Peter's proclamation? How did the people respond? (vv.9−10)

> "Solomon's Portico was a covered walkway formed by rows of columns supporting a roof and open on the inner side facing the center of the temple complex. Located on the east side of the Court of the Gentiles, it was a very public area. The Temple grounds adjacent to the Portico of Solomon would have been approximately four football fields in size which could have easily provided room for several thousand church members."
> *From the NET Bible*

5. How did Peter use this miracle to point to Jesus, their Messiah, in Acts 3:11−13?

6. What words are used to describe Jesus and what realities does Peter make clear? (vv. 13−16)

> "True repentance is admitting that what God says is true, and because it is true, to change our mind about our sins and about the Savior."
> ~ Warren Weirsbe

7. Peter's tone changed in verse 17. What did Peter encourage his listeners to do in verse 19 and why?

8. What promises does Peter remind his Jewish audience of in verses 24−26?

9. The Holy Spirit is not named in chapter 3, but we know He is there. In the verses below, underline what Scripture says the Holy Spirit does for us.

"But the Helper, the Holy Spirit, whom the Father will send in My name, He will teach you all things, and bring to your remembrance all that I said to you." John 14:26

"In Him, you also, after listening to the message of truth, the gospel of your salvation—having also believed, you were sealed in Him with the Holy Spirit of promise..." Ephesians 1:13

"In the same way the Spirit also helps our weakness; for we do not know how to pray as we should, but the Spirit Himself intercedes for us with groanings too deep for words; 27 and He who searches the hearts knows what the mind of the Spirit is, because He intercedes for the saints according to the will of God." Romans 8:26–27

"He saved us, not on the basis of deeds which we have done in righteousness, but according to His mercy, by the washing of regeneration and renewing by the Holy Spirit..." Titus 3:5

"But the fruit of the Spirit is love, joy, peace, patience, kindness, goodness, faithfulness, gentleness, self-control; against such things there is no law." Galatians 5:22–23

10. What evidence do you see of the Holy Spirit working in Acts 3:1–26?

STUDY TWO | Acts 4:1–14
Peter Testifies Before the Religious Leaders

The exchange in this passage must have felt familiar to Peter and John. Jesus had many times gone toe-to-toe with the religious elite in their attempts to shut down His ministry, and here they see His teaching lives on through His disciples. Peter might have crumbled before these intimidating men without the Holy Spirit's power sustaining his heart and mind. The last time he saw the high priest was from a distance, as Peter stood near a charcoal fire and repeatedly denied his Lord. But, on this day, the restored fisherman-turned-evangelist stood strong, and reminded these men that while they are ones who rejected salvation, it's not too late to lay a foundation in Christ.

___

1 As they were speaking to the people, the priests and the captain of the temple guard and the Sadducees came up to them, **2** being greatly disturbed because they were teaching the people and proclaiming in Jesus the resurrection from the dead. **3** And they laid hands on them and put them in jail until the next day, for it was already evening. **4** But many of those who had heard the message believed; and the number of the men came to be about five thousand.

5 On the next day, their rulers and elders and scribes were gathered together in Jerusalem; **6** and Annas the high priest was there, and Caiaphas and John and Alexander, and all who were of high-priestly descent. **7** When

Empowered: The Amazing Church of Jesus Christ

they had placed them in the center, they began to inquire, "By what power, or in what name, have you done this?" **8** Then Peter, filled with the Holy Spirit, said to them, "Rulers and elders of the people, **9** if we are on trial today for a benefit done to a sick man, as to how this man has been made well, **10** let it be known to all of you and to all the people of Israel, that by the name of Jesus Christ the Nazarene, whom you crucified, whom God raised from the dead— by this name this man stands here before you in good health. **11** He is the STONE WHICH WAS REJECTED by you, THE BUILDERS, but WHICH BECAME THE CHIEF CORNER stone. **12** And there is salvation in no one else; for there is no other name under heaven that has been given among men by which we must be saved." **13** Now as they observed the confidence of Peter and John and understood that they were uneducated and untrained men, they were amazed, and began to recognize them as having been with Jesus. **14** And seeing the man who had been healed standing with them, they had nothing to say in reply.

---

1. The priests, captain of the temple guard, and the Sadducees are seen for the first time in Acts in verse 1. What was their state of mind and what were their specific concerns? (v. 2)

2. What happened to Peter, John, and the Church in vv.3–4?

3. How is the contrast of events in Acts 4:3–4 a picture of what persecution does for the people of God? How do these verses encourage you?

> The Sadducees were the theological liberals of the day, and more political than religious. They denied the afterlife, the idea of any sort of resurrection, and the existence of angels and demons. Culturally, they were an aristocratic class connected with everything going on in the temple in Jerusalem. They tended to be wealthy and held powerful positions, including that of chief priests and high priest, and they held the majority of the 70 seats of the ruling council called the Sanhedrin. *(From www.gotquestions.org)*

4. We see familiar names in verses 5–6. Where have we seen these men before (John 18:13, 24)?

5. What were these religious leaders trying to determine? (v. 7)

6. What does Scripture teach us about the power of Jesus' name? Underline the instances of "the name of the Lord" below and draw an arrow to what His name accomplishes.

"The name of the Lord is a strong tower; the righteous runs into it and is safe." Proverbs 18:10

"There is none like You, O Lord; You are great, and great is Your name in might." Jeremiah 10:6

"The seventy returned with joy, saying, 'Lord, even the demons are subject to us in Your name.'" Luke 10:17

"...for 'Whoever will call on the name of the Lord will be saved.'" Romans 10:13

"For this reason also, God highly exalted Him, and bestowed on Him the name which is above every name, so that at the name of Jesus every knee will bow, of those who are in heaven and on earth and under the earth, and that every tongue will confess that Jesus Christ is Lord, to the glory of God the Father." Philippians 2:9–11

7. Briefly summarize how Peter answered the Sanhedrin's question in Acts 4:8–12. What is the only way for mankind to be saved?

8. What did the religious leaders observe about Peter and John in verse 13? What impact did that have on these leaders? How is 1 Corinthians 1:26–29 a commentary on this scene?

"For consider your calling, brethren, that there were not many wise according to the flesh, not many mighty, not many noble; but God has chosen the foolish things of the world to shame the wise, and God has chosen the weak things of the world to shame the things which are strong, and the base things of the world and the despised God has chosen, the things that are not, so that He may nullify the things that are, so that no man may boast before God."

9. What was the formerly lame man doing in Acts 4:14? How did the Sanhedrin respond to his presence?

10. What does Scripture say happens when we, like Peter and John, trust in the Lord? Choose at least ONE verse below and record your response.

Psalm 28:7   Isaiah 26:3
Proverbs 29:25   Jeremiah 17:7–8

STUDY THREE | Acts 4:15−31
The Believers Pray Boldly

The Sanhedrin—left speechless by the work of the Spirit they witnessed—sent Peter and John away with a command to keep quiet. And in return, the body of Christ gathered as one to worship and petition their Father in heaven. What a glorious response to a test of faith! Believers exalted the Lord and identified with Christ as they began to realize what it might be like to share in His suffering. The temptation to appeal for comfort was cast aside; these men and women were ready to count the cost and asked for a fearless faith instead. Heaven answered with an undeniable sign of favor and Spirit-filled supply for the work to continue.

---

15 But when they had ordered them to leave the Council, they began to confer with one another, **16** saying, "What shall we do with these men? For the fact that a noteworthy miracle has taken place through them is apparent to all who live in Jerusalem, and we cannot deny it. **17** But so that it will not spread any further among the people, let us warn them to speak no longer to any man in this name." **18** And when they had summoned them, they commanded them not to speak or teach at all in the name of Jesus. **19** But Peter and John answered and said to them, "Whether it is right in the sight of God to give heed to you rather than to God, you be the judge; **20** for we cannot stop speaking about what we have seen and heard." **21** When they had threatened them further, they let them go (finding no basis on which to punish them) on account of the people, because they were all glorifying God for what had happened; **22** for the man was more than forty years old on whom this miracle of healing had been performed.

23 When they had been released, they went to their own companions and reported all that the chief priests and the elders had said to them. **24** And when they heard this, they lifted their voices to God with one accord and said, "O Lord, it is You who MADE THE HEAVEN AND THE EARTH AND THE SEA, AND ALL THAT IS IN THEM, **25** who by the Holy Spirit, through the mouth of our father David Your servant, said,

'WHY DID THE GENTILES RAGE,
AND THE PEOPLES DEVISE FUTILE THINGS?
26 'THE KINGS OF THE EARTH TOOK THEIR STAND,
AND THE RULERS WERE GATHERED TOGETHER
AGAINST THE LORD AND AGAINST HIS CHRIST.'

27 For truly in this city there were gathered together against Your holy servant Jesus, whom You anointed, both Herod and Pontius Pilate, along with the Gentiles and the peoples of Israel, **28** to do whatever Your hand and Your purpose predestined to occur. **29** And now, Lord, take note of their threats, and grant that Your bond-servants may speak Your word with all confidence, **30** while You extend Your hand to heal, and signs and wonders take place through the name of Your holy servant Jesus." **31** And when they had prayed, the place where they had gathered together was shaken, and they were all filled with the Holy Spirit and began to speak the word of God with boldness.

---

1. At this point in time, Peter had preached two sermons, each time to crowds of ordinary men and women. As a result, more than 8,000 people were added to the body of Christ. Peter preaches a third sermon in Acts 4:8–12 to an elite group of religious leaders. How did they respond in verse 17–18?

2. Based on their discussion recorded in verses 15–16, what predicament did the Council find themselves in?

3. How Peter and John respond to the order given in verses 17–18? (vv. 19–20)

4. How does this encounter between Peter, John, and the Council encourage or challenge you?

5. Where did Peter and John go upon release and what did they do? (v. 23)

6. Their prayer is recorded in verses 24–30. Read it and note:

   What did they ask for?

   What didn't they ask for?

   How was their prayer answered in verse 31?

7. What do you learn about perseverance and suffering from this prayer?

8. Sharing your faith requires boldness, whether it's in a time of suffering like Peter and John or sitting across the table at lunch with a friend. What does Scripture say about what godly boldness looks like? In what circumstances are we told to be bold?

"The Lord is my light and my salvation; whom shall I fear? The Lord is the defense of my life; whom shall I dread?" Psalm 27:1

"On the day I called, You answered me; You made me bold with strength in my soul." Psalm 138:3

"...and pray on my behalf, that utterance may be given to me in the opening of my mouth, to make known with boldness the mystery of the gospel, for which I am an ambassador in chains; that in proclaiming it I may speak boldly, as I ought to speak." Ephesians 6:19–20

"...but after we had already suffered and been mistreated in Philippi, as you know, we had the boldness in our God to speak to you the gospel of God amid much opposition." 1 Thessalonians 2:2

"Therefore let us draw near with confidence to the throne of grace, so that we may receive mercy and find grace to help in time of need." Hebrews 4:16

STUDY FOUR | Acts 4:32–5:16
Unity and Deception in the Church

Our passage opens with a picture of the attitude and actions that build up the Church. And in the same breath, we are given a glimpse of the darkness that seeks to tear it down. Just as generous grace is a fountain of living water to our souls, hypocrisy and pride are poisons that pervade. They are toxic to our faith and fatal to our unity, dividing as they conquer. This event in the Church's early history serves to warn believers then and now, as it shines light on the sin that lurks in all our hearts. We see that fear and awe added a measure of gravity to the young and growing Church, but it did not snuff out the mission Jesus set in motion. Signs and wonders continued, and faith was strengthened as Christ demonstrated His passion to keep His Bride holy and pure.

32 And the congregation of those who believed were of one heart and soul; and not one of them claimed that anything belonging to him was his own, but all things were common property to them. 33 And with great power the apostles were giving testimony to the resurrection of the Lord Jesus, and abundant

grace was upon them all. **34** For there was not a needy person among them, for all who were owners of land or houses would sell them and bring the proceeds of the sales **35** and lay them at the apostles' feet, and they would be distributed to each as any had need.

36 Now Joseph, a Levite of Cyprian birth, who was also called Barnabas by the apostles (which translated means Son of Encouragement), **37** and who owned a tract of land, sold it and brought the money and laid it at the apostles' feet.

5 **1** But a man named Ananias, with his wife Sapphira, sold a piece of property, **2** and kept back some of the price for himself, with his wife's full knowledge, and bringing a portion of it, he laid it at the apostles' feet. **3** But Peter said, "Ananias, why has Satan filled your heart to lie to the Holy Spirit and to keep back some of the price of the land? **4** While it remained unsold, did it not remain your own? And after it was sold, was it not under your control? Why is it that you have conceived this deed in your heart? You have not lied to men but to God." **5** And as he heard these words, Ananias fell down and breathed his last; and great fear came over all who heard of it. **6** The young men got up and covered him up, and after carrying him out, they buried him.

7 Now there elapsed an interval of about three hours, and his wife came in, not knowing what had happened. **8** And Peter responded to her, "Tell me whether you sold the land-for such and such a price?" And she said, "Yes, that was the price." **9** Then Peter said to her, "Why is it that you have agreed together to put the Spirit of the Lord to the test? Behold, the feet of those who have buried your husband are at the door, and they will carry you out as well." **10** And immediately she fell at his feet and breathed her last, and the young men came in and found her dead, and they carried her out and buried her beside her husband. **11** And great fear came over the whole church, and over all who heard of these things.

12 At the hands of the apostles many signs and wonders were taking place among the people; and they were all with one accord in Solomon's portico. **13** But none of the rest dared to associate with them; however, the people held them in high esteem. **14** And all the more believers in the Lord, multitudes of men and women, were constantly added to their number, **15** to such an extent that they even carried the sick out into the streets and laid them on cots and pallets, so that when Peter came by at least his shadow might fall on any one of them. **16** Also the people from the cities in the vicinity of Jerusalem were coming together, bringing people who were sick or afflicted with unclean spirits, and they were all being healed.

---

1. Based on verses 32–35, what words would you use to describe the attitude and actions of the early Church?

Empowered: The Amazing Church of Jesus Christ

2. Who are we introduced to and what do we learn about him in verses 36–37?

3. We meet a married couple in Acts 5:1. What do you notice about their actions in verses 1–2 that is different from the description of Barnabas' gift in 4:37?

4. What did Peter discern about Ananias and Sapphira's "offering" and what might be the purpose of his question to Ananias? (vv.3–4)

5. Three hours later, Sapphira stops by. (v.7) What was Peter's indictment of her in verse 9?

6. What does this illustrate and what is the antidote? Read the scriptures below.

"Do not quench the Spirit." 1 Thessalonians 5:19

"Let no one say when he is tempted, 'I am being tempted by God'; for God cannot be tempted by evil, and He Himself does not tempt anyone. But each one is tempted when he is carried away and enticed by his own lust. Then when lust has conceived, it gives birth to sin; and when sin is accomplished, it brings forth death. Do not be deceived my beloved brethren." James 1:13–16

"But I say, walk by the Spirit, and you will not carry out the desire of the flesh." Galatians 5:16

7. What does it mean to walk in the Spirit?

8. Ananias and Sapphira's hypocrisy and deception to the church are examples of hidden or secret sin. What does the Bible say about secret sins? Underline the consequences. Use a highlighter to emphasize the results of confession and repentance.

"Who can discern his errors? Acquit me of hidden faults. Also keep back Your servant from presumptuous sins; let them not rule over me; then I will be blameless, and I shall be acquitted of great transgression." Psalm 19:12–13

"If I regard wickedness in my heart, the Lord will not hear; but certainly God has heard; He has given heed to the voice of my prayer." Psalm 66:18–19

"When I kept silent about my sin, my body wasted away through my groaning all day long. For day and night Your hand was heavy upon me; my vitality was drained away as with the fever heat of summer. *Selah.* I acknowledged my sin to You, and my iniquity I did not hide; I said, 'I will confess my transgressions to the Lord'; and You forgave the guilt of my sin." Psalm 32:3–5

"He who conceals his transgressions will not prosper, but he who confesses and for-sakes them will find compassion." Proverbs 28:13

"Woe to those who deeply hide their plans from the Lord, and whose deeds are done in a dark place, and they say, 'Who sees us?' or 'Who knows us?'" Isaiah 29:15

9. Ananias and Sapphira gave to the church with impure motives. What does the Bible teach us about the motives that inspire our giving in the verses below?

    "Each one must do just as he has purposed in his heart, not grudgingly or under compulsion, for God loves a cheerful giver. And God is able to make all grace abound to you, so that always having all sufficiency in everything, you may have an abundance for every good deed; as it is written, 'He scattered abroad, he gave to the poor, His righteousness endures forever.' Now He who supplies seed to the sower and bread for food will supply and multiply your seed for sowing and increase the harvest of your righteousness; you will be enriched in everything for all liberality, which through us is producing thanksgiving to God." 2 Corinthians 9:7–11

10. How does this help you evaluate your giving practices?

STUDY FIVE | Acts 5:17–42 | "Fighting Against God"

The religious leaders were frustrated by their inability to contain the apostles. Even prison could not hold these men or their message of Life. And now, the Council had murder on their minds. A respected Pharisee presented a case for the leaders to consider, calling to mind other rebellions that had failed. Their examples of failure provided assurance that self-serving revolts were an exercise in futility. But if something greater was, in fact, behind this movement, then the priest and all those with him would be the ones guilty of defying God. The apostles left the assembly persecuted and afflicted, but not struck down or destroyed, and rejoiced that sharing in His suffering also meant sharing in His glory.

Empowered: The Amazing Church of Jesus Christ

17 But the high priest rose up, along with all his associates (that is the sect of the Sadducees), and they were filled with jealousy. **18** They laid hands on the apostles and put them in a public jail. **19** But during the night an angel of the Lord opened the gates of the prison, and taking them out he said, **20** "Go, stand and speak to the people in the temple the whole message of this Life." **21** Upon hearing this, they entered into the temple about daybreak and began to teach.

Now when the high priest and his associates came, they called the Council together, even all the Senate of the sons of Israel, and sent orders to the prison house for them to be brought. **22** But the officers who came did not find them in the prison; and they returned and reported back, **23** saying, "We found the prison house locked quite securely and the guards standing at the doors; but when we had opened up, we found no one inside." **24** Now when the captain of the temple guard and the chief priests heard these words, they were greatly perplexed about them as to what would come of this. **25** But someone came and reported to them, "The men whom you put in prison are standing in the temple and teaching the people!" **26** Then the captain went along with the officers and proceeded to bring them back without violence (for they were afraid of the people, that they might be stoned).

27 When they had brought them, they stood them before the Council. The high priest questioned them, **28** saying, "We gave you strict orders not to continue teaching in this name, and yet, you have filled Jerusalem with your teaching and intend to bring this man's blood upon us." **29** But Peter and the apostles answered, "We must obey God rather than men. **30** The God of our fathers raised up Jesus, whom you had put to death by hanging Him on a cross. **31** He is the one whom God exalted to His right hand as a Prince and a Savior, to grant repentance to Israel, and forgiveness of sins. **32** And we are witnesses of these things; and so is the Holy Spirit, whom God has given to those who obey Him."

33 But when they heard this, they were cut to the quick and intended to kill them. **34** But a Pharisee named Gamaliel, a teacher of the Law, respected by all the people, stood up in the Council and gave orders to put the men outside for a short time. **35** And he said to them, "Men of Israel, take care what you propose to do with these men. **36** For some time ago Theudas rose up, claiming to be somebody, and a group of about four hundred men joined up with him. But he was killed, and all who followed him were dispersed and came to nothing. **37** After this man, Judas of Galilee rose up in the days of the census and drew away some people after him; he too perished, and all those who followed him were scattered. **38** So in the present case, I say to you, stay away from these men and let them alone, for if this plan or action is of men, it will be overthrown; **39** but if it is of God, you will not be able to overthrow them; or else you may even be found fighting against God."

40 They took his advice; and after calling the apostles in, they flogged them and ordered them not to speak in the name of Jesus, and then released them. **41** So they went on their way from the presence of the Council, rejoicing that they had been considered worthy to suffer shame for His name. **42** And every day, in the temple and from house to house, they kept right on teaching and preaching Jesus as the Christ.

---

1. What did the high priest and his cohorts do to the apostles; and what was heaven's response? (vv.17–20)

2. How did the apostles respond in verse 21a?

3. How did the opposition respond in verse 21b?

 4. Read verses 5:22–24. What parallels to the resurrection of Christ do you see in this scene? (Matthew 27:59–66)

5. The apostles willingly returned to the Council in verses 25–26. What two accusations did the high priest charge them with in verse 28?

6. The miraculous prison escape was indeed a sign and wonder pointing to Christ and could have been heeded by the religious leaders. Why do you think their eyes and hearts remained closed?

 7. Read and observe Acts 5:29–32. This is another call to repentance and offer of grace. What do you learn about God, Jesus, and the Holy Spirit?

Empowered: The Amazing Church of Jesus Christ

8. Describe Gamaliel and explain the steps he used to develop his case. (vv. 34–39)

9. Why do you think the Council responded as they did in verse 40?

"Jewish flogging was done with leather whips. They gave 13 lashes on the chest and 26 on the back for a total of 39 lashes (40 minus one)." From *The Moody Bible Commentary*, based on Deuteronomy 25:3.

WEEK 3 TEACHING NOTES

Empowered: *The Amazing Church of Jesus Christ*

Acts 6–8:3

The Early Church in Judea and Samaria

We meet two central figures in Acts and Church history this week: Stephen, a devoted servant of the Gospel and God's people, and Saul, an up-and-coming religious leader zealous to destroy the movement associated with the crucified carpenter's Son.

Stephen stood out for his wisdom, faith, and powerful teaching. He was dynamic yet humbly walked in the Spirit, performing signs and wonders that drew the people away from religion and into a relationship.

Saul was trying to make a name for himself. The religious circles he ran in wanted to annihilate this new group of misguided heretics. These "believers" were multiplying and organized. Things were getting out of hand.

Stephen used an unexpected platform to walk his Jewish accusers through the history of Israel's neglect and rebellion and God's unwavering faithfulness. His speech incited rage among his hearers and ended in grievous loss to the Church. And there in the shadows, Saul was giving his blessing to the bloodshed.

The stoning of Stephen was only the beginning of a mass persecution of the Church. But God's purposes will not be thwarted; the ends of the earth will be reached. And He will use not only words and wonders to do it. God will use tragedy, persecution, and even transform defiant doubters into suffering servants to carry His message of life and hope to the world.

KEY VERSE

"And on that day a great persecution began against the church in Jerusalem, and they were all scattered throughout the regions of Judea and Samaria, except the apostles."

ACTS 8:1B

STUDY ONE | Acts 6:1–15
Stephen's Appointment and Arrest

This chapter of Acts opens with the rising Church's first internal conflict. As with all dissension, this presented God's people with the opportunity to strengthen or divide. One man among the newly chosen leadership stood out in word and deed, clearly anointed by God and filled with His Spirit. But his ministry attracted the enemy, and many of his peers organized to oppose him. The darkness in their hearts blinded them to the truth that burned like a beacon before their eyes.

---

1 Now at this time while the disciples were increasing in number, a complaint arose on the part of the Hellenistic Jews against the native Hebrews, because their widows were being overlooked in the daily serving of food. **2** So the twelve summoned the congregation of the disciples and said, "It is not desirable for us to neglect the word of God in order to serve tables. **3** Therefore, brethren, select from among you seven men of good reputation, full of the Spirit and of wisdom, whom we may put in charge of this task. **4** But we will devote ourselves to prayer and to the ministry of the word." **5** The statement found approval with the whole congregation; and they chose Stephen, a man full of faith and of the Holy Spirit, and Philip, Prochorus, Nicanor, Timon, Parmenas and Nicolas, a proselyte from Antioch. **6** And these they brought before the apostles; and after praying, they laid their hands on them.

    7 The word of God kept on spreading; and the number of the disciples continued to increase greatly in Jerusalem, and a great many of the priests were becoming obedient to the faith.

    8 And Stephen, full of grace and power, was performing great wonders and signs among the people. **9** But some men from what was called the Synagogue of the Freedmen, including both Cyrenians and Alexandrians, and some from Cilicia and Asia, rose up and argued with Stephen. **10** But they were unable to cope with the wisdom and the Spirit with which he was speaking. **11** Then they secretly induced men to say, "We have heard him speak blasphemous words against Moses and against God." **12** And they stirred up the people, the elders and the scribes, and they came up to him and dragged him away and brought him before the Council. **13** They put forward false witnesses who said, "This man incessantly speaks against this holy place and the Law; **14** for we have heard him say that this Nazarene, Jesus, will destroy this place and alter the customs which Moses handed down to us." **15** And fixing their gaze on him, all who were sitting in the Council saw his face like the face of an angel.

---

1. Verse 1 presents a big picture of the state of the Church at the time. What was happening to the Church and *within* the Church?

2. How did the apostles decide to resolve the issue described in verse 1? (vv. 2–4)

According to Smith's Bible Dictionary, Hellenistic Jew is "a term applied in the New Testament to Greek-speaking or 'Grecian' Jews. The Hellenists as a body included not only the proselytes of Greek (or foreign) parentage, but also those Jews who, by settling in foreign countries, had adopted the prevalent form of the current Greek civilization, and with it the use of the common Greek dialect."

Empowered: The Amazing Church of Jesus Christ

3. How did this reorganization affect the overall ministry of the Gospel? (v. 7)

4. Stephen is first introduced in verse 5 and he is seen again in verse 8. How does the author, Luke, describe him?

5. Note from verse 9 who opposed Stephen and his ministry. How does verse 10 say Stephen was able to face his opposition? (see also Matthew 5:10–12; Luke 21:16–19)

6. What was Stephen accused of in Acts 6:11, 13–14?

7. What did the opposition do in response? (vv. 11–14)

A DEEPER LOOK

The word "deacon" comes from the Greek word "diakoneo," which is translated "serve" in the New Testament. Acts 6:1–6 gives us a picture of the first selection of this group of servant leaders and notably places a high premium on their inward qualities rather than their outward abilities.

Look back at the passage and observe three things:

1. Who was summoned to choose the seven men? (v. 2)

2. The qualifications required to serve. (v. 3)

3. How the church responded to this change. (v.5)

Read 1 Timothy 3:8–13. What are the qualifications for this office outlined in this passage? Re-read verse 13 and record the blessing for those who serve the Church in this capacity.

STUDY TWO | Acts 7:1–34
Stephen Speaks to the Sanhedrin

Stephen stood in the middle of a "fiery trial" (1 Peter 4:12–13)—opposed and accused by the religious leaders of the day and called on the spot to defend his ministry and his God. By the power of the Holy Spirit, he delivered one of the most eloquent discourses in Scripture of God's dealings with Israel. This is the longest sermon in Acts, demonstrating the many different ways, places, and times God worked through His servants to graciously draw His people to Himself.

----

1 The high priest said, "Are these things so?"

2 And he said, "Hear me, brethren and fathers! The God of glory appeared to our father Abraham when he was in Mesopotamia, before he lived in Haran, **3** and said to him, 'Leave your country and your relatives, and come into the land that I will show you.' **4** Then he left the land of the Chaldeans and settled in Haran. From there, after his father died, God had him move to this country in which you are now living. **5** But He gave him no inheritance in it, not even a foot of ground, and yet, even when he had no child, He promised that He would give it to him as a possession, and to his descendants after him. **6** But God spoke to this effect, that his descendants would be aliens in a foreign land, and that they would be enslaved and mistreated for four hundred years. **7** 'And whatever nation to which they will be in bondage I Myself will judge,' said God, 'and after that they will come out and serve Me in this place.' **8** And He gave him the covenant of circumcision; and so Abraham became the father of Isaac, and circumcised him on the eighth day; and Isaac became the father of Jacob, and Jacob of the twelve patriarchs.

9 "The patriarchs became jealous of Joseph and sold him into Egypt. Yet God was with him,**10** and rescued him from all his afflictions, and granted him favor and wisdom in the sight of Pharaoh, king of Egypt, and he made him governor over Egypt and all his household.

Empowered: The Amazing Church of Jesus Christ

11 "Now a famine came over all Egypt and Canaan, and great affliction with it, and our fathers could find no food. **12** But when Jacob heard that there was grain in Egypt, he sent our fathers there the first time. **13** On the second visit Joseph made himself known to his brothers, and Joseph's family was disclosed to Pharaoh. **14** Then Joseph sent word and invited Jacob his father and all his relatives to come to him, seventy-five persons in all. **15** And Jacob went down to Egypt and there he and our fathers died. **16** From there they were removed to Shechem and laid in the tomb which Abraham had purchased for a sum of money from the sons of Hamor in Shechem.

17 "But as the time of the promise was approaching which God had assured to Abraham, the people increased and multiplied in Egypt, **18** until there arose another king over Egypt who knew nothing about Joseph. **19** It was he who took shrewd advantage of our race and mistreated our fathers so that they would expose their infants and they would not survive. **20** It was at this time that Moses was born; and he was lovely in the sight of God, and he was nurtured three months in his father's home. **21** And after he had been set outside, Pharaoh's daughter took him away and nurtured him as her own son. **22** Moses was educated in all the learning of the Egyptians, and he was a man of power in words and deeds. **23** But when he was approaching the age of forty, it entered his mind to visit his brethren, the sons of Israel. **24** And when he saw one of them being treated unjustly, he defended him and took vengeance for the oppressed by striking down the Egyptian. **25** And he supposed that his brethren understood that God was granting them deliverance through him, but they did not understand. **26** On the following day he appeared to them as they were fighting together, and he tried to reconcile them in peace, saying, 'Men, you are brethren, why do you injure one another?' **27** But the one who was injuring his neighbor pushed him away, saying, 'Who made you a ruler and judge over us? **28** You do not mean to kill me as you killed the Egyptian yesterday, do you?' **29** At this remark, Moses fled and became an alien in the land of Midian, where he became the father of two sons.

30 "After forty years had passed, an angel appeared to him in the wilderness of Mount Sinai, in the flame of a burning thorn bush. **31** When Moses saw it, he marveled at the sight; and as he approached to look more closely, there came the voice of the Lord: **32** 'I am the God of your fathers, the God of Abraham and Isaac and Jacob.' Moses shook with fear and would not venture to look. **33** But the Lord said to him, 'Take off the sandals from your feet, for the place on which you are standing is holy ground. **34** I have certainly seen the oppression of My people in Egypt and have heard their groans, and I have come down to rescue them; come now, and I will send you to Egypt.'

---

1. Stephen gave a thorough summary of Israel's spiritual history in response to the high priest's question in Acts 7:1. What were the promises God made to Abraham in verses 5–7?

> The time period Stephen covers in his speech is approximately 3,000 years.

2. How do we see these promises fulfilled in Joseph and the patriarchs? (vv. 9–16)

3. How do we see these promises fulfilled in slavery in Egypt? (vv. 17–19)

4. How do we see these promises fulfilled in the life of Moses? (vv. 20–34)

5. What might have been Stephen's purpose in encouraging his "brothers and fathers" to remember these stories of their history?

6. What did they learn about their history and themselves?

7. What did they learn about their God?

8. What was the message for them in that moment?

9. How can you apply this deeply theological recounting of the spiritual history of Israel in your life right now?

A DEEPER LOOK

Stephen spoke of the God who had been faithful for generations to the people of Israel. As you reflect on your life, recall the ways God has shown Himself faithful to you as well. If it helps, think of your life in specific time frames, like decades. What specific ways have you seen God's faithfulness to you in those seasons?

Take a few moments right now to praise God for His unchanging character, purposes, and Word to us—that He was the same then as now and forevermore!

STUDY THREE | Acts 7:35–53
Stephen Indicts His Hearers

After the exegesis came the indictment, of both their past and present sin of rejection. Stephen did not mince words with his audience, charging them with following in the footsteps of their fathers, willingly walking in their own kind of wilderness. They were idolaters and unrighteous with blind eyes and hardened hearts. Emboldened by the Spirit's power and aware of all that was at stake, Stephen ended his discourse with the sharpest judgement of all: *not only did you murder God's messengers, you murdered the One who was sent to save you.*

---

35 "This Moses whom they disowned, saying, 'Who made you a ruler and a judge?' is the one whom God sent to be both a ruler and a deliverer with the help of the angel who appeared to him in the thorn bush. 36 This man led them out, performing wonders and signs in the land of Egypt and in the Red Sea and in the wilderness for forty years. 37 This is the Moses who said to the sons of Israel, 'God will raise up for you a prophet like me from your brethren.' 38 This is the one who was in the congregation in the wilderness together with the angel who was speaking to him on Mount Sinai, and who was with our fathers; and he received living oracles to pass on to you. 39 Our fathers were unwilling to be obedient to him, but repudiated him and in their hearts turned back to Egypt, 40 saying to Aaron, 'Make for us gods who will go before us; for this Moses who led us out of the land of Egypt—we do not know what happened to him.' 41 At that time they made a calf and brought a sacrifice to the idol, and were rejoicing in the works of their hands. 42 But God turned away and delivered them up to serve the host of heaven; as it is written in the book of the prophets, 'It was not to Me that you offered victims and sacrifices forty years in the wilderness, was it, O house of Israel? 43 You also took along the tabernacle of Moloch and the star of the god Rompha, the images which you made to worship. I also will remove you beyond Babylon.'

44 "Our fathers had the tabernacle of testimony in the wilderness, just as He who spoke to Moses directed him to make it according to the pattern which he had seen. 45 And having received it in their turn, our fathers brought it in with Joshua upon dispossessing the nations whom God drove out before our fathers, until the time of David. 46 David found favor in God's sight, and asked that he might find a dwelling place for the God of Jacob. 47 But it was Solomon who built a house for Him. 48 However, the Most High does not dwell in houses made by human hands; as the prophet says:

49 'Heaven is My throne,
And earth is the footstool of My feet;
What kind of house will you build for Me?' says the Lord,

'Or what place is there for My repose?
50 'Was it not My hand which made all these things?'

51 "You men who are stiff-necked and uncircumcised in heart and ears are always resisting the Holy Spirit; you are doing just as your fathers did. 52 Which one of the prophets did your fathers not persecute? They killed those who had previously announced the coming of the Righteous One, whose betrayers and murderers you have now become; 53 you who received the law as ordained by angels, and yet did not keep it."

---

1. What do you observe about the sinfulness of man in verses 35–41?

2. What was God's response to sin in verses 42–43?

3. Based on the accusations previously made in Acts 6:11–14, why did Stephen spend so much time describing Israel's historical relationship with Moses in Acts 7:5–41?

4. The Jews also accused Stephen of speaking against "this holy place"—the Temple—in Acts 6:13. What point did Stephen make about God's dwelling place in Acts 7:44–50?

5. What errors in thinking was Stephen pointing out? Read the verse below to help inform your answer.

"But will God indeed dwell on the earth? Behold, heaven and the highest heaven cannot contain You, how much less this house which I have built!" (1 Kings 8:27)

6. Why do you think the audience did not connect the dots between the history Stephen was presenting and the current situation?

Empowered: The Amazing Church of Jesus Christ

7. Look up Mark 7:9 and 13. How do these verses help clarify their problem?

8. Stephen ended his speech with an indictment against all within earshot of his words. How did he describe their spiritual condition? (Acts 7:51)

9. What was the sinful attitude displayed in verses 52–53?

A DEEPER LOOK

Review the wise warning of Gamaliel recorded in Acts 5:34–39. The religious leaders of the day acquiesced for that moment but, ultimately, did not take those words to heart. As a result, life- and history-altering sins were committed.

What does the Bible tell us about the importance of cultivating a teachable spirit? Choose at least ONE of the passages below and record what you learn.

Psalm 1:1–6   Proverbs 21:11
Psalm 143:10   Proverbs 29:1
Proverbs 15:31–33   1 Corinthians 2:12–14

Choose one verse from those listed to memorize and use as a prayer to God, asking Him to cultivate a teachable spirit in you. Write it here.

STUDY | Acts 7:54–8:3
FOUR | Stephen Dies, Saul Appears, and the Church Scatters

The depravity of man and the glory of God were each on display in the death of Stephen. He suffered a brutal death at the hands of a savage mob. But even as his life met its violent end, Stephen rested in the glorious presence of his Savior. This passage reveals what we are capable of both with and without the indwelling Holy Spirit. This passage is also our first glimpse of Saul, a man God would ultimately use to change the history of the world. In the moment, Stephen's death had a devastating effect, scattering the Church as they fled persecution. But looking back, we can see it was a victory, because God used His faithful servant to spread the Gospel, just as He promised.

54 Now when they heard this, they were cut to the quick, and they began gnashing their teeth at him. **55** But being full of the Holy Spirit, he gazed intently into heaven and saw the glory of God, and Jesus standing at the right hand of God; **56** and he said, "Behold, I see the heavens opened up and the Son of Man standing at the right hand of God." **57** But they cried out with a loud voice, and covered their ears and rushed at him with one impulse. **58** When they had driven him out of the city, they began stoning him; and the witnesses laid aside their robes at the feet of a young man named Saul. **59** They went on stoning Stephen as he called on the Lord and said, "Lord Jesus, receive my spirit!" **60** Then falling on his knees, he cried out with a loud voice, "Lord, do not hold this sin against them!" Having said this, he fell asleep.

8 Saul was in hearty agreement with putting him to death. And on that day a great persecution began against the church in Jerusalem, and they were all scattered throughout the regions of Judea and Samaria, except the apostles. **2** Some devout men buried Stephen, and made loud lamentation over him. **3** But Saul began ravaging the church, entering house after house, and dragging off men and women, he would put them in prison.

 1. How did the people respond to Stephen's speech? (vv. 54, 57–58)

 2. Who appeared for the first time in Scripture as Stephen is stoned in Acts 7:57–58; 8:1? What is his role?

3. How did Stephen's experience of death illustrate Psalm 23:4?

 4. What event took place as a direct result of the martyrdom of Stephen? (v. 8:1)

5. What actions did Saul take after Stephen's death? (v. 3)

> The Greek word "rushed" in verse 57 is the same word used to describe the way the herd of pigs rushed off the cliff in the Gadarenes after Jesus cast demons out of the possessed men in Matthew 8:32.

> Foxe's *Book of Martyrs* records that "about two thousand Christians, with Nicanor, one of the seven deacons, suffered martyrdom during the persecution that arose about Stephen."

> Webster's dictionary defines *martyr* as "a person who voluntarily suffers death as the penalty of witnessing to and refusing to renounce a religion." *Martyr* is the Greek word for *witness*.

6. How does Luke describe the contrast between the impact Stephen's death and Saul's life had on the Church in verses 2–3?

7. We all have a story of someone we know—maybe someone we love—whose life was seemingly cut short, perhaps in their prime. Consider the arc of events in Acts so far—from the coming of the Holy Spirit to Stephen's death, a time period that scholars believe was approximately two years.

   What immediate emotional, psychological, and/or spiritual impact might this turn of events have had on the followers of Christ?

A DEEPER LOOK

Using a dictionary, look up and define the words below.

Suffer

Trials

Opposition

Harassment

Persecution

What does the Bible teach us about facing persecution? Choose at least ONE verse below and write the truths about persecution of believers that you learn.

John 15:18–20   Philippians 1:12–14
Romans 8:35–39   James 1:12

Thinking about the words you defined, how is persecution different from suffering? Based on these verses, what does true persecution look like?

When we contend—or fight—for our faith, we can expect some form of opposition. Remembering how Stephen responded in Acts 7:55–60, where should our focus be when we are opposed?

STUDY FIVE | The World Turned Upside Down

We are the informed readers of Acts 6–8, seeing victories and tragedies in the Church intermingled, and understanding what the men and women of the time could not: God was at work not only in their blessings—the growth of the Church, the establishment of governance, the emergence of passionate leaders—but through their incomprehensible suffering as well.

1. Consider Stephen's teaching through the Old Testament in Acts 7:1–53. What was the response of the people to his teaching that day? (vv. 54, 57–58)

2. How did it impact the mission of the Church? (8:1)

3. How does this challenge or support your view about the importance of the Old Testament in increasing faith and leading some to salvation?

4. Both Peter and Stephen were called and equipped by God to the same mission: spread the Gospel and make disciples. Would the world describe each outcome as a success or failure? Explain.

5. What do these two stories teach us about how God measures "success" and "failure?"

6. How does God's definition of success compare to your own?

Empowered: The Amazing Church of Jesus Christ

7. Look at the passages on the next page to read and record what you learn about how the Lord defines true success in this world and for eternity. Paraphrase the verses and then assign a key word that helps summarize the behaviors that determine success in God's eyes.

Reference	Paraphrase the Verse	Assign a Key Word for Verse
1 Kings 2:3–4	Keep the commands of the Lord so you may succeed.	Obey
2 Kings 18:6–7		
Proverbs 3:1–6		
Jeremiah 17:7–8		
Mark 12:28–34		
Luke 16:10–11		

8. Are there any adjustments to your thinking, lifestyle, or expectations that you need to make moving forward?

WEEK 4 TEACHING NOTES

Map of Paul's Conversion and Early Ministry

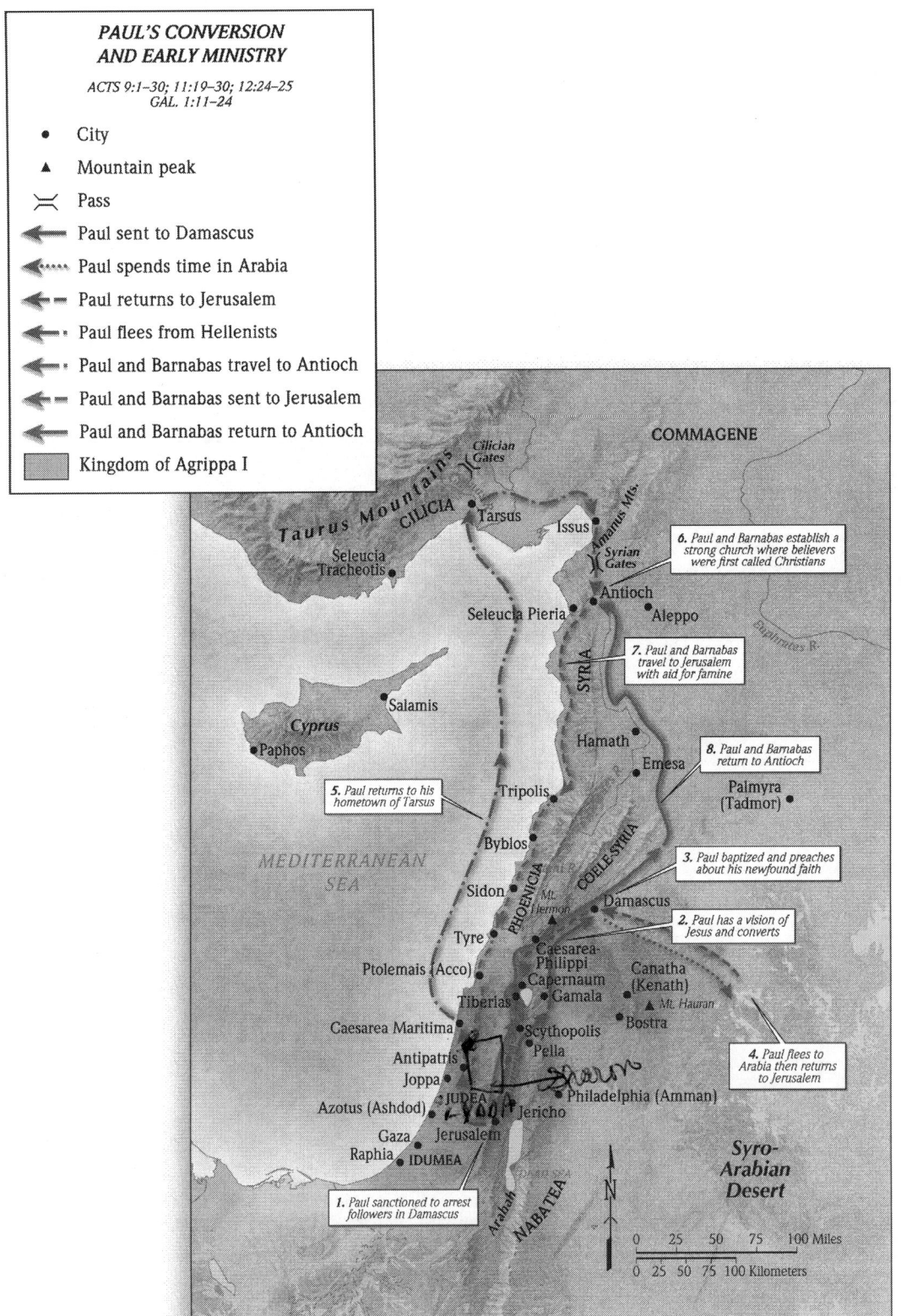

PAUL'S CONVERSION AND EARLY MINISTRY

ACTS 9:1–30; 11:19–30; 12:24–25
GAL. 1:11–24

- • City
- ▲ Mountain peak
- ⋈ Pass
- ← Paul sent to Damascus
- ← Paul spends time in Arabia
- ← Paul returns to Jerusalem
- ← Paul flees from Hellenists
- ← Paul and Barnabas travel to Antioch
- ← Paul and Barnabas sent to Jerusalem
- ← Paul and Barnabas return to Antioch
- ▪ Kingdom of Agrippa I

COMMAGENE

Cilician Gates

Taurus Mountains

CILICIA

Tarsus

Issus

Amanus Mts.

Syrian Gates

6. Paul and Barnabas establish a strong church where believers were first called Christians

Seleucia Tracheotis

Antioch

Aleppo

Seleucia Pieria

Euphrates R.

SYRIA

7. Paul and Barnabas travel to Jerusalem with aid for famine

Salamis

Hamath

Emesa

Palmyra (Tadmor)

8. Paul and Barnabas return to Antioch

Cyprus

Paphos

5. Paul returns to his hometown of Tarsus

Tripolis

3. Paul baptized and preaches about his newfound faith

MEDITERRANEAN SEA

Byblos

COELE-SYRIA

Sidon

Mt. Hermon

Damascus

2. Paul has a vision of Jesus and converts

PHOENICIA

Tyre

Caesarea-Philippi

Capernaum

Canatha (Kenath)

Ptolemais (Acco)

Gamala

▲ Mt. Hauran

Tiberias

Bostra

Caesarea Maritima

Scythopolis

Pella

4. Paul flees to Arabia then returns to Jerusalem

Antipatris

Joppa

JUDEA

Philadelphia (Amman)

Azotus (Ashdod)

Jericho

Gaza

Jerusalem

Syro-Arabian Desert

Raphia

IDUMEA

N

1. Paul sanctioned to arrest followers in Damascus

Arabah

NABATEA

0   25   50   75   100 Miles

0 25 50 75 100 Kilometers

Acts 8:4–9:43

The Conversion of Saul

The hatred was like a fire inside him, and it burned hotter with every step. He'd never felt such clarity. These followers of "the Way" may have fled Jerusalem, but he would track them down and make them answer for their profane teaching. Like Elijah's judgment of the prophets of Baal, those who had forsaken God's law must be punished.

There were no words for what happened next. An indescribable brightness—clearly visible but impossible to see. And then a voice he didn't yet recognize invaded his soul with truth that felt like a stream in the desert. The transformation was God-ordained: three days in darkness brought a dead man to life. And, as a new creation, Saul would be an instrument the hand of God would use to change the world.

The conversion of Saul is one of many miraculous stories of salvation we see this week. A race of people hated for centuries by the Jews are welcomed into Christ's growing Church. A man, miles from nowhere, receives a supernatural and personal visit from a willing disciple and hears the truth he was longing for.

The infant Church was just opening its eyes to the power of grace. And these stories illustrate that, by His Spirit working through His people, the ministry of Jesus had only just begun.

KEY VERSE

"But the Lord said to him, 'Go, for he is a chosen instrument of Mine, to bear My name before the Gentiles and kings and the sons of Israel; for I will show him how much he must suffer for My name's sake.'"

Acts 9:15–16

STUDY ONE | Acts 8:4–25
| The Gospel Goes to Samaria

This week opens with a beautiful picture of the grassroots effort to spread the Gospel. Like seeds in the wind, the persecuted Jewish converts scattered to carry the message of life and hope to the world. These ordinary men and women were compelled by their call and burdened for the lost and found many eager to receive the Word. Philip travelled to Samaria and helped bridge a cultural divide with grace and truth. Peter joined him and confronted the difference between a false and saving faith. Salvation is a gift available to all, but there will always be hearts hard to penetrate, and those who prefer an attitude of avoidance rather than submission and repentance.

---

4 Therefore, those who had been scattered went about preaching the word. **5** Philip went down to the city of Samaria and began proclaiming Christ to them. **6** The crowds with one accord were giving attention to what was said by Philip, as they heard and saw the signs which he was performing. **7** For in the case of many who had unclean spirits, they were coming out of them shouting with a loud voice; and many who had been paralyzed and lame were healed. **8** So there was much rejoicing in that city.

9 Now there was a man named Simon, who formerly was practicing magic in the city and astonishing the people of Samaria, claiming to be someone great; **10** and they all, from smallest to greatest, were giving attention to him, saying, "This man is what is called the Great Power of God." **11** And they were giving him attention because he had for a long time astonished them with his magic arts. **12** But when they believed Philip preaching the good news about the kingdom of God and the name of Jesus Christ, they were being baptized, men and women alike. **13** Even Simon himself believed; and after being baptized, he continued on with Philip, and as he observed signs and great miracles taking place, he was constantly amazed.

14 Now when the apostles in Jerusalem heard that Samaria had received the word of God, they sent them Peter and John, **15** who came down and prayed for them that they might receive the Holy Spirit. **16** For He had not yet fallen upon any of them; they had simply been baptized in the name of the Lord Jesus. **17** Then they began laying their hands on them, and they were receiving the Holy Spirit. **18** Now when Simon saw that the Spirit was bestowed through the laying on of the apostles' hands, he offered them money, **19** saying, "Give this authority to me as well, so that everyone on whom I lay my hands may receive the Holy Spirit." **20** But Peter said to him, "May your silver perish with you, because you thought you could obtain the gift of God with money! **21** You have no part or portion in this matter, for your heart is not right before God. **22** Therefore repent of this wickedness of yours, and pray the Lord that, if possible, the intention of your heart may be forgiven you. **23** For I see that you are in the gall of bitterness and in the bondage of iniquity." **24** But Simon answered and said, "Pray to the Lord for me yourselves, so that nothing of what you have said may come upon me." **25** So, when they had solemnly testified and spoken the word of the Lord, they started back to Jerusalem, and were preaching the gospel to many villages of the Samaritans.

Empowered: The Amazing Church of Jesus Christ

1. We saw the effects of Saul's persecution in Acts 8:3: "But Saul began ravaging the church, entering house after house, and dragging off men and women, he would put them in prison." What is another result of the persecution of the Church seen in verses 4–5?

2. What are the human and supernatural responses to Philip's ministry seen in Acts 8:6–8?

> In order to dilute the nation, the king of Assyria mixed Jews with foreigners during Israel's exile. The result was the intermarriage of Jew and Gentile, and the Samaritan race was born. Samaritans embraced a mixture of Judaism and idolatry, creating irreconcilable animosity between the two. See 2 Kings 17:22–24 for the biblical background.

3. A demonic distraction had been entrenched among the people in this city for a long time. What do we learn about this in Acts 8:9–13?

> Philip is first seen in Acts 6:5 when he was appointed one of the Church's first deacons. These men were described as being "of good reputation, full of the Spirit and of wisdom…" (Acts 6:3).

4. Peter and John are sent from Jerusalem to Samaria. How would the presence and experience of Peter and John in Samaria help the believers in Jerusalem accept the believers in Samaria and the Samaritans accept the apostolic authority in Jerusalem? (vv. 14–17)

> "God didn't bring the apostles to Samaria to bestow the Holy Spirit but to witness the Samaritans receiving the Holy Spirit. The Lord delayed the falling of the Holy Spirit for the apostles' benefit, to assure them that He had accepted the Samaritans' belief and had made them full-fledged brothers and sisters in the kingdom." ~ Chuck Swindoll's *Living Insights* Commentary on Acts

5. What was Simon's response to the ministry of Peter and John to the believers in Samaria? (Acts 8:18–19)

6. What does Simon's request reveal about his belief? James 2:19 gives us a fuller understanding — "You believe that God is one. You do well; the demons also believe, and shudder."

7. Based on his request, who did Simon think could receive the Holy Spirit? How does that differ from what the Bible teaches?

Acts 2:38

Titus 3:5–6

1 John 4:12–13

8. What indictment and instruction did Peter pronounce against Simon? What was Simon's response? (Acts 8:20–24)

9. It seems the apostles took advantage of every opportunity to carry out the mission that Jesus called them to. What ways do we see they did this in verse 25?

> The Greek word Luke uses in this strong curse against Simon means *utter and hopeless loss of all that gives worth to existence.* Peter was essentially saying, "You and your money are both going to hell if you continue on this destructive path." All is not lost if Simon repents.

STUDY TWO | Acts 8:26–40
The Ethiopian's Journey to Faith

After proclaiming the good news of Jesus to crowds in Samaria, Philip obediently took the road less traveled to find one God-fearing man who was seeking truth without a guide. How interesting that this man did not hear the Gospel while in Jerusalem, the religious center of the world at the time, or from the gathering of God's people at the temple where he had gone to worship. Instead, he learned of Jesus on a desert road from a servant of God who was submitted to the leading of the Holy Spirit. Obedient hearts can make all the difference in the lives of those on the journey to faith.

---

26 But an angel of the Lord spoke to Philip saying, "Get up and go south to the road that descends from Jerusalem to Gaza." (This is a desert road.) **27** So he got up and went; and there was an Ethiopian eunuch, a court official of Candace, queen of the Ethiopians, who was in charge of all her treasure; and he had come to Jerusalem to worship, **28** and he was returning and sitting in his chariot, and was reading the prophet Isaiah. **29** Then the Spirit said to Philip, "Go up and join this chariot." **30** Philip ran up and heard him reading Isaiah the prophet, and said, "Do you understand what you are reading?" **31** And he said, "Well, how could I, unless someone guides me?" And he invited Philip to come up and sit with him. **32** Now the passage of Scripture which he was reading was this:
"He was led as a sheep to slaughter;
And as a lamb before its shearer is silent,

So He does not open His mouth.
33 "In humiliation His judgment was taken away;
Who will relate His generation?
For His life is removed from the earth."

34 The eunuch answered Philip and said, "Please tell me, of whom does the prophet say this? Of himself or of someone else?" 35 Then Philip opened his mouth, and beginning from this Scripture he preached Jesus to him. 36 As they went along the road they came to some water; and the eunuch said, "Look! Water! What prevents me from being baptized?" 37 [and Philip said, "If you believe with all your heart, you may." And he answered and said, "I believe that Jesus Christ is the Son of God."] 38 And he ordered the chariot to stop; and they both went down into the water, Philip as well as the eunuch, and he baptized him. 39 When they came up out of the water, the Spirit of the Lord snatched Philip away; and the eunuch no longer saw him, but went on his way rejoicing. 40 But Philip found himself at Azotus, and as he passed through he kept preaching the gospel to all the cities until he came to Caesarea.

---

1. The angel of the Lord told Philip to get up and go. Where was he to go and who did he meet there? (vv. 26–28)

2. Considering this contrast, what questions come to your mind related to this drastic change in location about God's plan for Philip and even the Gospel?

3. How do the Lord's words in Isaiah 55:8–9 below help you think about this?

"'For My thoughts are not your thoughts, nor are your ways My ways,'" declares the Lord.
"'For as the heavens are higher than the earth, so are My ways higher than your ways and My thoughts than your thoughts.'"

4. Describe the encounter Philip had after he joined the eunuch in verses 30–31.

> In the East at this time in history, eunuchs commonly were in charge of the bed chambers (or harems) in a royal court. They often rose to positions of great power and trust. The term also refers generally to a court official. There is no conclusive evidence that all eunuchs were castrated.

5. The passage the eunuch was reading was Isaiah 53:7–8. Read the entirety of Isaiah 53. This is one of the most Messianic chapters in the Bible. The Ethiopian eunuch asked Philip to tell him who the prophet is talking about. (Acts 8:34) Based on your reading of Isaiah 53, what had he learned about Jesus so far?

> "It is not a prophecy, it is a gospel." ~ St. Augustine, describing Isaiah 53

6. Is there a passage of Scripture that first illuminated Christ and the Gospel to you or has there been someone in your life with knowledge of Scripture that illuminated Christ to you?

7. What was the Ethiopian's response to Philip's teaching from Scripture? (Acts 8:36–38)

8. How did the eunuch's response to faith differ from that of Simon, the sorcerer?

9. A supernatural event happens in verse 39. How might that have validated the eunuch's life-changing conversation with Philip, a stranger he met in the middle of nowhere?

10. What does this passage say to you about the lengths the Father will go to reach the world with His grace and truth? How does this encourage you in your life and relationship with unbelievers?

STUDY THREE | Acts 9:1–19a
The Light Shines into Darkness

Saul polluted the very air around him with cruelty and hate. His passion for destruction poisoned his mind and fueled a murderous mission. While the Lord sent Philip to save the eunuch in the desert, this lost soul would receive His personal attention. Saul was on his way to wipe out anyone who called on Jesus' name when he encountered the Light that opened his blind heart to truth. While Saul sat in darkness, God sent a reluctant disciple to dispense amazing grace, witnessing Saul's heart transformed and zeal redeemed.

1 Now Saul, still breathing threats and murder against the disciples of the Lord, went to the high priest, **2** and asked for letters from him to the synagogues at Damascus, so that if he found any belonging to the Way, both men and women, he might bring them bound to Jerusalem. **3** As he was traveling, it happened that he was approaching Damascus, and suddenly a light from heaven flashed around him; **4** and he fell to the ground and heard a voice saying to him, "Saul, Saul, why are you persecuting Me?" **5** And he said, "Who are You, Lord?" And He said, "I am Jesus whom you are persecuting, **6** but get up and enter the city, and it will be told you what you must do." **7** The men who traveled with him stood speechless, hearing the voice but seeing no one. **8** Saul got up from the ground, and though his eyes were open, he could see nothing; and leading him by the hand, they brought him into Damascus. **9** And he was three days without sight, and neither ate nor drank.

10 Now there was a disciple at Damascus named Ananias; and the Lord said to him in a vision, "Ananias." And he said, "Here I am, Lord." **11** And the Lord said to him, "Get up and go to the street called Straight, and inquire at the house of Judas for a man from Tarsus named Saul, for he is praying, **12** and he has seen in a vision a man named Ananias come in and lay his hands on him, so that he might regain his sight." **13** But Ananias answered, "Lord, I have heard from many about this man, how much harm he did to Your saints at Jerusalem; **14** and here he has authority from the chief priests to bind all who call on Your name." **15** But the Lord said to him, "Go, for he is a chosen instrument of Mine, to bear My name before the Gentiles and kings and the sons of Israel; **16** for I will show him how much he must suffer for My name's sake." **17** So Ananias departed and entered the house, and after laying his hands on him said, "Brother Saul, the Lord Jesus, who appeared to you on the road by which you were coming, has sent me so that you may regain your sight and be filled with the Holy Spirit." **18** And immediately there fell from his eyes something like scales, and he regained his sight, and he got up and was baptized; **19** and he took food and was strengthened.

---

1. Who was Saul and what was he doing? (vv. 1–3a)

2. How would Saul have credibility for this kind of behavior? (see Philippians 3:5–6)

3. What happened to Saul "as he was approaching Damascus" in Acts 9:3–6?

4. How did Saul respond in Acts 9:8–9?

5. How do the following verses help you understand what Jesus was communicating to Saul?

"For thus says the Lord of hosts, 'After glory He has sent me against the nations which plunder you, for he who touches you, touches the apple of His eye.'" Zechariah 2:8

"The King will answer and say to them, 'Truly I say to you, to the extent that you did it to one of these brothers of Mine, even the least of them, you did it to Me.'" Matthew 25:40

"...for no one ever hated his own flesh, but nourishes and cherishes it, just as Christ also does the church, because we are members of His body." Ephesians 5:29–30

6. How did the Lord speak to Ananias and what did He tell him to do? (Acts 9:10–12)

7. What did Ananias know about Saul that made him so hesitant to follow God's command? (vv. 13–14)

8. Saul's mission in life was outlined for us in verses 1–2. What is the Lord's plan for Saul as revealed in verses 15–16?

9. Saul wasn't going to suffer as payback or punishment. Saul was going to suffer for the glory of Christ and the salvation of others: "...always carrying about in the body the dying of Jesus, so that the life of Jesus also may be manifested in our body." (2 Corinthians 4:10)

Read the verses below and answer: What happens to a person's sin—every cruel threat, murderous thought, and evil intent—the moment he repents and receives Jesus as his Savior?

"As far as the east is from the west, so far has He removed our transgressions from us." Psalm 103:12

"Lo, for my own welfare I had great bitterness; it is You who has kept my soul from the pit of nothingness, For You have cast all my sins behind Your back." Isaiah 38:17

"He will again have compassion on us; He will tread our iniquities under foot. Yes, You will cast all their sins into the depths of the sea." Micah 7:19

"If we confess our sins, He is faithful and righteous to forgive us our sins and to cleanse us from all unrighteousness." 1 John 1:9

10. How did the Lord use Ananias in Saul's conversion and commission? How do you think this experience would have been faith-building for Ananias? (Acts 9:17–18)

STUDY FOUR | Acts 9:19b–31
A New Man on a New Mission

The impact of Saul's radical transformation was seen immediately, and it was hard to believe. The seeds of fear were already planted throughout the body of Christ, and it would take time to uproot them. But Saul proved his newfound faith by boldly professing the Gospel he once rejected wherever there were ears to hear. A hand of friendship helped make inroads for Saul in the Church, providing clarity and comfort. While Saul entered Damascus helpless and in darkness, he left assisted by his brothers in Christ with his eyes wide open and heart full of light.

---

19 Now for several days he was with the disciples who were at Damascus, **20** and immediately he began to proclaim Jesus in the synagogues, saying, "He is the Son of God." **21** All those hearing him continued to be amazed, and were saying, "Is this not he who in Jerusalem destroyed those who called on this name, and who had come here for the purpose of bringing them bound before the chief priests?" **22** But Saul kept increasing in strength and confounding the Jews who lived at Damascus by proving that this Jesus is the Christ.

23 When many days had elapsed, the Jews plotted together to do away with him, **24** but their plot became known to Saul. They were also watching the gates day and night so that they might put him to death; **25** but his disciples took him by night and let him down through an opening in the wall, lowering him in a large basket.

26 When he came to Jerusalem, he was trying to associate with the disciples; but they were all afraid of him, not believing that he was a disciple. **27** But

Barnabas took hold of him and brought him to the apostles and described to them how he had seen the Lord on the road, and that He had talked to him, and how at Damascus he had spoken out boldly in the name of Jesus. **28** And he was with them, moving about freely in Jerusalem, speaking out boldly in the name of the Lord. **29** And he was talking and arguing with the Hellenistic Jews; but they were attempting to put him to death. **30** But when the brethren learned of it, they brought him down to Caesarea and sent him away to Tarsus.

31 So the church throughout all Judea and Galilee and Samaria enjoyed peace, being built up; and going on in the fear of the Lord and in the comfort of the Holy Spirit, it continued to increase.

---

1. In verses 19–21 who was Saul with and why were they amazed by what he was saying?

2. What do we learn about Paul's perspective on his life from the verses below?

   Galatians 1:13–14

   1 Timothy 1:12–16

3. How did the Jews decide to "handle" Saul in Acts 9:23–24?

4. Because the Jews had decided to kill him, Saul escaped Damascus through a hole in the wall of the city with the help of his disciples. (v. 25) How do verses 23–25 reflect the effectiveness of Saul's ministry and the love that the believers now had for him?

5. There is movement between verses 25 and 26 from Damascus to Jerusalem, but the time frame is important to note. Read Galatians 1:15–23 for background on this time period. What do you learn about Saul and his preparation for a lifetime of serving the Lord?

What is an apostle?
." James – Jesus brother an apostle?

Empowered: The Amazing Church of Jesus Christ

6. When he arrived in Jerusalem, how did the disciples there respond to Saul as a new creation in Christ? (Acts 9:26)

7. What specific ways did Barnabas help Saul in his newfound calling? (v. 27)

8. Remember the meaning of *Barnabas*: son of encouragement. How would his intercession on Saul's behalf have been an encouragement to Saul?

9. Tell of a time when someone advocated for you—or you stepped in to vouch for someone else's reputation or character? What difference did that selfless act make in the lives of those involved?

STUDY FIVE | Acts 9:32–43
Peter, the Itinerant Preacher

Peter, filled with the Holy Spirit, traveled from town to town, speaking of abundant life and demonstrating the Spirit's power as he was led. Much like his Savior and Friend, Jesus, Peter would heal a broken body then teach a captivated audience about the sickness in their souls and the truth that would set them free. Powerful testimony of a healing miracle made its way ten miles down the road to a group of grieving friends. They called on Peter to restore a life, and he came with a message of hope as well. The timing of this tragedy was perfectly ordained by our sovereign God, who placed Peter close enough to work a miracle—bringing glory to His name and growing His kingdom.

---

32 Now as Peter was traveling through all those regions, he came down also to the saints who lived at Lydda. 33 There he found a man named Aeneas, who had been bedridden eight years, for he was paralyzed. 34 Peter said to him, "Aeneas, Jesus Christ heals you; get up and make your bed." Immediately he got up. 35 And all who lived at Lydda and Sharon saw him, and they turned to the Lord.

36 Now in Joppa there was a disciple named Tabitha (which translated in Greek is called Dorcas); this woman was abounding with deeds of kindness and charity which she continually did. 37 And it happened at that time that she fell sick and died; and when they had washed her body, they laid it in an upper room. 38 Since Lydda was near Joppa, the disciples, having heard that Peter was there, sent two men to him, imploring him, "Do not delay in coming to us." 39 So Peter arose and went with them. When he arrived, they brought him

into the upper room; and all the widows stood beside him, weeping and showing all the tunics and garments that Dorcas used to make while she was with them. **40** But Peter sent them all out and knelt down and prayed, and turning to the body, he said, "Tabitha, arise." And she opened her eyes, and when she saw Peter, she sat up. **41** And he gave her his hand and raised her up; and calling the saints and widows, he presented her alive. **42** It became known all over Joppa, and many believed in the Lord. **43** And Peter stayed many days in Joppa with a tanner named Simon.

---

1. How had Peter been carrying out the mission of Acts 1:8? (v. 32)

2. In verses 34–35 when Peter healed Aeneas in the name of Jesus, Peter told him to do something Aeneas hadn't been able to do in nearly a decade. What was it and how would it impact the paralytic's life?

3. Peter's act of compassion for this man resulted in an even greater miracle "for all who lived at Lydda and Sharon." What was it? (Acts 9:35)

4. Describe the woman we meet and what happened to her. (vv. 36–37)

> Tabitha is the only woman in the New Testament explicitly named as a disciple.

5. What evidence can we see in verses 37–39 that show Tabitha was loved by those around her?

> "The placing of her body in an upper room is unusual. This action may well express the faith and hope that she can be raised from the dead, as usually burial took place before sunset in Judaism." Dr. Darrell Bock, *Baker Exegetical Commentary on the New Testament: Acts*

6. Tabitha was known for her continual and abundant acts of kindness and compassion for others. What does the Bible say about how our works and our faith are intertwined?

"Let your light shine before men in such a way that they may see your good works, and glorify your Father who is in heaven." Matthew 5:16

Empowered: The Amazing Church of Jesus Christ

"Therefore, my beloved brethren, be steadfast, immovable, always abounding in the work of the Lord, knowing that your toil is not in vain in the Lord." 1 Corinthians 15:58

"So then, while we have opportunity, let us do good to all people, and especially to those who are of the household of the faith." Galatians 6:10

"For we are His workmanship, created in Christ Jesus for good works, which God prepared beforehand so that we would walk in them." Ephesians 2:10

"For just as the body without the spirit is dead, so also faith without works is dead." James 2:26

7. How was Tabitha brought back to life? (v. 40)

8. How do we know Jesus is the One who accomplished the miracles at Lydda and Joppa and that Peter was simply the vessel? (vv. 34, 40; see also Luke 8:54–55)

 9. What was the impact of this miracle on the people of Joppa? (Acts 9:42)

10. Luke mentions one last detail at the end of Acts 9: Peter stayed in Joppa with a man named Simon, who was a tanner. A tanner is someone who converts animal hides into leather. Tanners were technically considered unclean by the Jews because of Leviticus 11:39–40.

The Book of Acts: Witnesses to the World by Steven Ger says this about the profession:

> "Tanners usually worked in or near their homes, and primarily because of the associated odor, those employed as tanners had to live a minimum of twenty-five yards outside the borders of a city. Jews ranked the occupation of tanning alongside those of prostitution, dung collecting, gambling and driving donkeys."

What is notable about Peter, a Jewish apostle, staying in the home of someone like Simon?

WEEK 5 TEACHING NOTES

Map of Gospel to the Gentiles

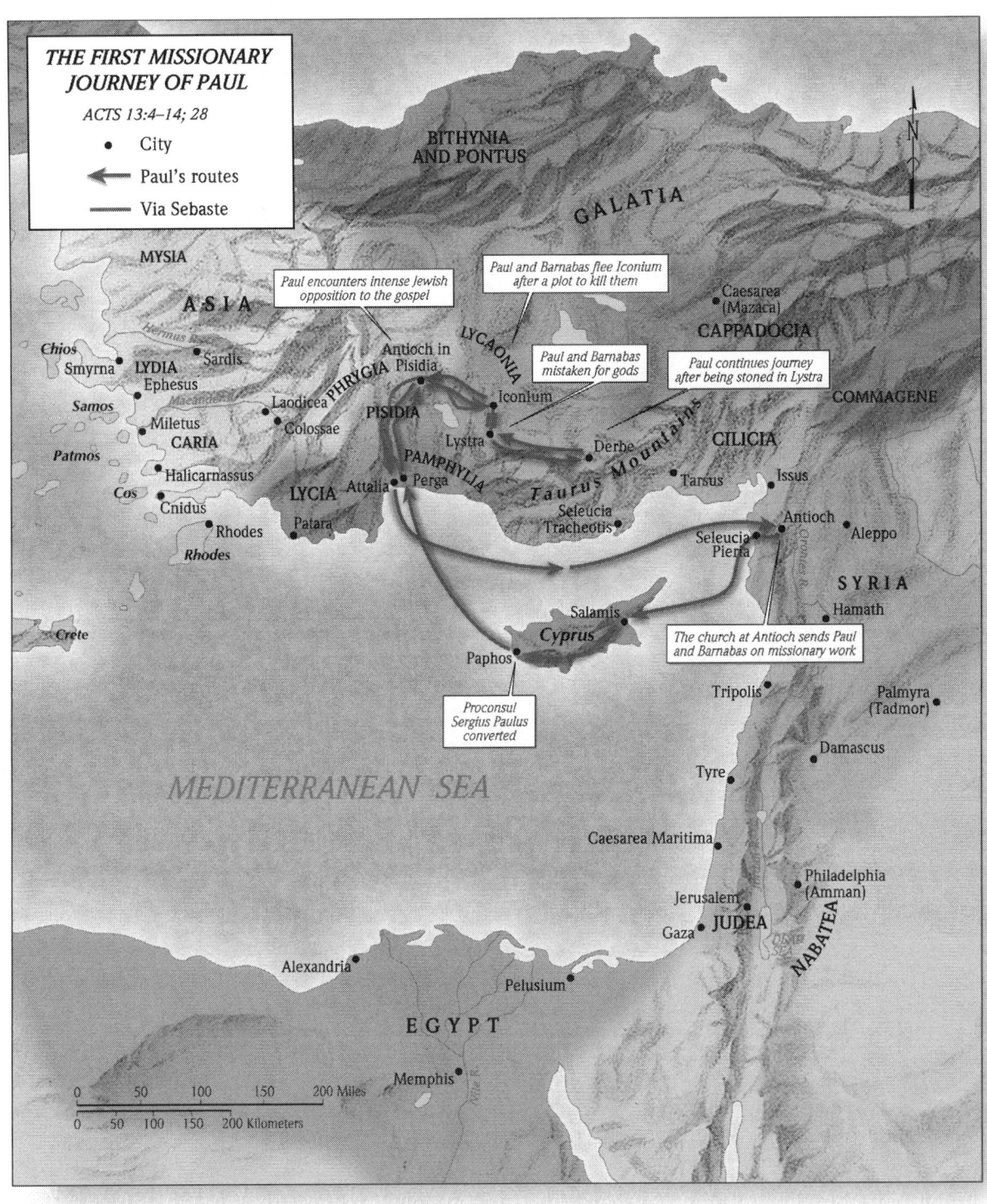

THE FIRST MISSIONARY JOURNEY OF PAUL

ACTS 13:4–14; 28

- • City
- ← Paul's routes
- — Via Sebaste

BITHYNIA AND PONTUS

GALATIA

MYSIA

ASIA

Paul encounters intense Jewish opposition to the gospel

Paul and Barnabas flee Iconium after a plot to kill them

Caesarea (Mazaca)

CAPPADOCIA

LYCAONIA

Chios
Smyrna
LYDIA
Sardis
Ephesus

Antioch in Pisidia

Paul and Barnabas mistaken for gods

Paul continues journey after being stoned in Lystra

COMMAGENE

Samos

Laodicea
PHRYGIA
Colossae
PISIDIA

Iconium

Miletus
CARIA

Lystra
Derbe

CILICIA

Patmos

Halicarnassus

PAMPHYLIA

Tarsus
Issus

Cos
Cnidus
LYCIA
Attalia
Perga

Taurus Mountains

Rhodes
Patara

Seleucia
Tracheotis

Antioch
Aleppo

Rhodes

Seleucia Pieria

SYRIA

Crete

Salamis

Hamath

Cyprus

The church at Antioch sends Paul and Barnabas on missionary work

Paphos

Proconsul Sergius Paulus converted

Tripolis

Palmyra (Tadmor)

MEDITERRANEAN SEA

Damascus

Tyre

Caesarea Maritima

Philadelphia (Amman)

Jerusalem
Gaza
JUDEA

NABATEA

Alexandria

Pelusium

EGYPT

0   50   100   150   200 Miles
0   50   100   150   200 Kilometers

Memphis

Week 5

Acts 10–12

The Gospel Goes to the Gentiles

The door to the Church swings wide open on one of the most important hinges in history in our passage for this week. The Gentiles, once avoided at all costs, are brought near through Christ, grafted into the Tree of Life, and adopted as sons and daughters into the family of God. The story of how this came to pass is told in such detail, there could be no doubt then or now that this was the hand and the will of God at work.

This seismic shift began with prayer, more than thirty miles and twenty-four hours apart, but both heaven-sent. Peter's physical hunger is met by a sheet carrying a revelation that is at once repulsive and intriguing to him. Peter's questions were answered when he obediently met with a spiritually hungry Gentile who knew his best efforts just weren't enough. An angel, a voice, and the Spirit directed the play-by-play as the plan of God unfolded for His Church and His children.

Acts' focus on Peter's ministry ends with his miraculous escape from prison and punishment exacted on a persecutor of God's people. And the word of God flourished like a strong vine in sunlight, reaching those near and far off with grace and truth.

KEY VERSE:

"...I most certainly understand now that God is not one to show partiality, but in every nation the man who fears Him and does what is right is welcome to Him."

ACTS 10:34–35

STUDY ONE | Acts 10:1–23a
A Vision from Heaven

A visit from an angel and an unappetizing vision upended expectations and revealed a revelation for Peter and a soldier who was seeking the Lord. This was the "hinge moment" in the life of the Church, opening eyes and hearts to a relationship no one at the time thought possible. This major shift in early doctrine did more than make room for more at the table. These events remind us that God is not limited by our rules or traditions, and that yielding to His will in faith is always more than enough. And when it comes to salvation, man's "goodness" will never outweigh the grace that forever tips the scales in our favor.

1 Now there was a man at Caesarea named Cornelius, a centurion of what was called the Italian cohort, **2** a devout man and one who feared God with all his household, and gave many alms to the Jewish people and prayed to God continually. **3** About the ninth hour of the day he clearly saw in a vision an angel of God who had just come in and said to him, "Cornelius!" **4** And fixing his gaze on him and being much alarmed, he said, "What is it, Lord?" And he said to him, "Your prayers and alms have ascended as a memorial before God. **5** Now dispatch some men to Joppa and send for a man named Simon, who is also called Peter; **6** he is staying with a tanner named Simon, whose house is by the sea." **7** When the angel who was speaking to him had left, he summoned two of his servants and a devout soldier of those who were his personal attendants, **8** and after he had explained everything to them, he sent them to Joppa.

9 On the next day, as they were on their way and approaching the city, Peter went up on the housetop about the sixth hour to pray. **10** But he became hungry and was desiring to eat; but while they were making preparations, he fell into a trance; **11** and he saw the sky opened up, and an object like a great sheet coming down, lowered by four corners to the ground, **12** and there were in it all kinds of four-footed animals and crawling creatures of the earth and birds of the air. **13** A voice came to him, "Get up, Peter, kill and eat!" **14** But Peter said, "By no means, Lord, for I have never eaten anything unholy and unclean." **15** Again a voice came to him a second time, "What God has cleansed, no longer consider unholy." **16** This happened three times, and immediately the object was taken up into the sky.

17 Now while Peter was greatly perplexed in mind as to what the vision which he had seen might be, behold, the men who had been sent by Cornelius, having asked directions for Simon's house, appeared at the gate; **18** and calling out, they were asking whether Simon, who was also called Peter, was staying there. **19** While Peter was reflecting on the vision, the Spirit said to him, "Behold, three men are looking for you. **20** But get up, go downstairs and accompany them without misgivings, for I have sent them Myself." **21** Peter went down to the men and said, "Behold, I am the one you are looking for; what is the reason for which you have come?" **22** They said, "Cornelius, a centurion, a righteous and God-fearing man well spoken of by the entire nation of the Jews, was divinely directed by a holy angel to send for you to come to his house and hear a message from you." **23** So he invited them in and gave them lodging.

---

1. A military leader named Cornelius is introduced in Acts 10:1–2.

What unusual event did Cornelius experience "about the ninth hour" (3 p.m.)? (v. 3)

2. The New Living Translation of the Bible explains that the phrase "memorial before God" (v. 4) means that, even though he is not a Jew, Cornelius' prayers and gifts to those in need had been received by God as an offering. How does Scripture describe the different kinds of offerings the Lord receives? Underline your answer in the verses below.

> A Roman centurion was a professional military officer who commanded a troop of 100 or more men. *Fausset's Bible Dictionary* notes that, "Good conduct was generally the cause of their promotion to the command" of a platoon of troops. A cohort would be made up of about 600 men who are part of a legion of 6,000.

"Therefore I urge you, brethren, by the mercies of God, to present your bodies a living and holy sacrifice, acceptable to God, which is your spiritual service of worship." Romans 12:1

"But I have received everything in full and have an abundance; I am amply supplied, having received from Epaphroditus what you have sent, a fragrant aroma, an acceptable sacrifice, well-pleasing to God." Philippians 4:18

"Through Him then, let us continually offer up a sacrifice of praise to God, that is, the fruit of lips that give thanks to His name. And do not neglect doing good and sharing, for with such sacrifices God is pleased." Hebrews 13:15–16

3. What does God's Word say to people like Cornelius? Think back on a time when you were either seeking the Lord for the first time, or where you purposed to know Him better and love Him more. How do the verses below stir your heart to seek more of your Savior?

"I love those who love me; and those who diligently seek me will find me." Proverbs 8:17

"How blessed are those who observe His testimonies, who seek Him with all their heart." Psalm 119:2

"You will seek Me and find Me when you search for Me with all your heart." Jeremiah 29:13

"Blessed are those who hunger and thirst for righteousness, for they shall be satisfied." Matthew 5:6

4. What was the instruction in verse 13 and how would you describe Peter's response in verse 14?

5. How can our partiality or biases (i.e., toward a certain faith tradition or practice or against a specific group of people) lead to legalism and/or discrimination?

6. Peter didn't even have time to digest this information before guests arrived in Acts 10:17–18. What instructions did the Holy Spirit give Peter in verses 19–20?

7. What did the Spirit say to Peter in verses 19-20 that the angel did not say to Cornelius in verse 5? Why might this "extra encouragement" have been necessary?

8. What else do we learn about Cornelius from his men in verse 22?

9. Why did the men say they had come? (v. 22) How did Peter respond? (v. 23)

A DEEPER LOOK

Read Ephesians 2:11–12. How are those outside the family of God described?

Read Ephesians 2:13–18. What has the blood of Christ accomplished for those who are "near" (the Jews) and those who are "far off" (the Gentiles)?

Take time now and ask God to reveal anything in your heart that might be considered a "dividing wall of hostility," (ESV) keeping you from engaging with others for the sake of the Gospel.

STUDY TWO | Acts 10:23b–48
The Gentile Pentecost

When Peter arrived in Caesarea, he encountered not just one Gentile but a house full!

This audience had drawn near to hear from God, but their hearts were still far from Him. And once Peter obediently crossed the barrier to openly meet with those considered "unclean," God's Spirit provided the faith that gave life. This moment marked the last time anyone would have to be excluded from fellowship on earth or denied access to the kingdom of God. The veil torn in two in the temple upon Christ's death on the cross made no distinction; it was an offer of grace to everyone who believes—"... for the same Lord is Lord of all, abounding in riches for all who call on Him..." (Romans 10:12)

Empowered: The Amazing Church of Jesus Christ

23 And on the next day he got up and went away with them, and some of the brethren from Joppa accompanied him. **24** On the following day he entered Caesarea. Now Cornelius was waiting for them and had called together his relatives and close friends. **25** When Peter entered, Cornelius met him, and fell at his feet and worshiped him. **26** But Peter raised him up, saying, "Stand up; I too am just a man." **27** As he talked with him, he entered and found many people assembled. **28** And he said to them, "You yourselves know how unlawful it is for a man who is a Jew to associate with a foreigner or to visit him; and yet God has shown me that I should not call any man unholy or unclean. **29** That is why I came without even raising any objection when I was sent for. So I ask for what reason you have sent for me."

30 Cornelius said, "Four days ago to this hour, I was praying in my house during the ninth hour; and behold, a man stood before me in shining garments, **31** and he said, 'Cornelius, your prayer has been heard and your alms have been remembered before God. **32** Therefore send to Joppa and invite Simon, who is also called Peter, to come to you; he is staying at the house of Simon the tanner by the sea.' **33** So I sent for you immediately, and you have been kind enough to come. Now then, we are all here present before God to hear all that you have been commanded by the Lord."

34 Opening his mouth, Peter said:

"I most certainly understand now that God is not one to show partiality, **35** but in every nation the man who fears Him and does what is right is welcome to Him. **36** The word which He sent to the sons of Israel, preaching peace through Jesus Christ (He is Lord of all)— **37** you yourselves know the thing which took place throughout all Judea, starting from Galilee, after the baptism which John proclaimed. **38** You know of Jesus of Nazareth, how God anointed Him with the Holy Spirit and with power, and how He went about doing good and healing all who were oppressed by the devil, for God was with Him. **39** We are witnesses of all the things He did both in the land of the Jews and in Jerusalem. They also put Him to death by hanging Him on a cross. **40** God raised Him up on the third day and granted that He become visible, **41** not to all the people, but to witnesses who were chosen beforehand by God, that is, to us who ate and drank with Him after He arose from the dead. **42** And He ordered us to preach to the people, and solemnly to testify that this is the One who has been appointed by God as Judge of the living and the dead. **43** Of Him all the prophets bear witness that through His name everyone who believes in Him receives forgiveness of sins."

44 While Peter was still speaking these words, the Holy Spirit fell upon all those who were listening to the message. **45** All the circumcised believers who came with Peter were amazed, because the gift of the Holy Spirit had been poured out on the Gentiles also. **46** For they were hearing them speaking with tongues and exalting God. Then Peter answered, **47** "Surely no one can refuse the water for these to be baptized who have received the Holy Spirit just as we did, can he?" **48** And he ordered them to be baptized in the name of Jesus Christ. Then they asked him to stay on for a few days.

1. What evidence do we see in verse 24 that tells us Cornelius was expecting to hear from the Lord, as He promised? Share a time when hope and expectant faith were on display in your life.

2. In verse 28 Peter begins by immediately addressing the "elephant in the room." What did Peter reveal about his change of heart in verses 28–29?

3. What do verses 34–35 tell us that Peter finally understands? How do the verses below give us further insight?

   Luke 24:47

   John 10:16

   John 12:32

   Romans 3:29–30

4. Circle the word "partiality" in Acts 10:34. Using a dictionary, define *partiality*. Read Romans 2:11. What does it say about God's position on partiality?

5. At times, we can be guilty of assigning certain prejudices to God, meaning, we tend to believe He thinks like we do—about certain groups of people or issues like social status, school choice, denominations, race, politics, etc.

   Do you believe Peter's statement about God in Acts 10:34? Why or why not? How do your prejudices—conscious and unconscious—get in the way of being able to see life from God's perspective?

6. Salvation is based on the person and work of Jesus Christ, only and alone. What did the Gentiles need to know about Jesus before they could receive Him as Savior? (vv. 36–43)

7. Cornelius is described in this chapter as a very good man. (vv. 2, 4, 22) But was his "goodness" enough to save him? How do we know that salvation isn't granted based only on being good or doing good? Look up the following verses:

"And there is salvation in no one else; for there is no other name under heaven that has been given among men by which we must be saved." Acts 4:12

"... for all have sinned and fall short of the glory of God ..." Romans 3:23

"For by grace you have been saved through faith; and that not of yourselves, it is the gift of God; not as a result of works, so that no one may boast." Ephesians 2:8–9

"And without faith it is impossible to please Him, for he who comes to God must believe that He is and that He is a rewarder of those who seek Him." Hebrews 11:6

8. How do we know that Cornelius and his household were saved that day? (Acts 10:44)

9. What evidence do we—along with Peter and the witnesses—see in verse 46 that the Holy Spirit had fallen on the Gentiles? What next step did Peter order? (vv. 47–48)

> Because of the many similarities to the coming of the Holy Spirit in Acts 2, scholars refer to this event as the Gentile Pentecost. Estimates on the timeline vary, but most believe this event occurred five to ten years after Acts 2:2–4.

10. Why might this group of new believers have wanted Peter to stay longer with them? (v. 48) How does 2 Peter 3:18 speak to this?

A DEEPER LOOK

Through the centuries, the prophets had born witness (Acts 10:43) about a promise that would ultimately be fulfilled. The fulfillment occurred in this passage and it was amazing to the Jews. (v. 45) What was the prophecy and promise fulfilled at this time?

Psalm 86:9

Isaiah 49:6

Isaiah 45:22

STUDY | Acts 11:1–18
THREE | The Church's Confirmation

After a myopic response to a miraculous event, Peter tells the story of the Gentiles' salvation for the third time and emphasized the transformation that occurred in his own heart as well. These ultra-conservative Jews never considered it possible that pagans could be made holy or that strangers could become brothers. But their acceptance proved that every heart can be made new. No one is named in Peter's third account, because this is really not about a man or meal. It's about the work and plan of God progressively unfolding, revealing just how wide and long and high and deep is the love of Christ.

---

1 Now the apostles and the brethren who were throughout Judea heard that the Gentiles also had received the word of God. **2** And when Peter came up to Jerusalem, those who were circumcised took issue with him, **3** saying, "You went to uncircumcised men and ate with them." **4** But Peter began speaking and proceeded to explain to them in orderly sequence, saying, **5** "I was in the city of Joppa praying; and in a trance I saw a vision, an object coming down like a great sheet lowered by four corners from the sky; and it came right down to me, **6** and when I had fixed my gaze on it and was observing it I saw the four-footed animals of the earth and the wild beasts and the crawling creatures and the birds of the air. **7** I also heard a voice saying to me, 'Get up, Peter; kill and eat.' **8** But I said, 'By no means, Lord, for nothing unholy or unclean has ever entered my mouth.' **9** But a voice from heaven answered a second time, 'What God has cleansed, no longer consider unholy.' **10** This happened three times, and everything was drawn back up into the sky. **11** And behold, at that moment three men appeared at the house in which we were staying, having been sent to me from Caesarea. **12** The Spirit told me to go with them without misgivings. These six brethren also went with me and we entered the man's house. **13** And he reported to us how he had seen the angel standing in his house, and saying, 'Send to Joppa and have Simon, who is also called Peter, brought here; **14** and he will speak words to you by which you will be saved, you and all your household.' **15** And as I began to speak, the Holy Spirit fell upon them just as He did upon us at the beginning. **16** And I remembered the word of the Lord, how He used to say, 'John baptized with water, but you will be baptized with the Holy Spirit.' **17** Therefore if God gave to them the same gift as He gave to us also after believing in the Lord Jesus Christ, who was I that I could stand in God's way?" **18** When they heard this, they quieted down and glorified God, saying, "Well then, God has granted to the Gentiles also the repentance that leads to life."

---

1. How did the "apostles and brethren" (Jewish Christians) receive the news that the Gentiles had accepted the message of the Gospel? (vv. 1–3)

   What example had Jesus set for Peter (and what had He been criticized for) in His ministry?

   Matthew 9:11

   Luke 5:30

2. How did Peter approach this emotional situation in Acts 11:4?

3. What did the angel promise Cornelius about Peter in verse 14?

4. What evidence does verse 15 provide that this promise was fulfilled?

5. The Holy Spirit brought the words of Jesus to mind to help build a bridge of acceptance in his heart to this new work of God. (v. 16) How has God's Word shown itself to be consistent, assuring, and reliable in your life? (In other words, how is God's Word better than feelings?) Remember:

   "Heaven and earth will pass away, but My words will not pass away." Matthew 24:35

"...for you have been born again not of seed which is perishable but imperishable, that is, through the living and enduring word of God." 1 Peter 1:23

"The grass withers, the flower fades, but the word of our God stands forever." Isaiah 40:8

6. Acts 11:18 can be considered irony. In acknowledging the Gentiles' receiving the gift of repentance, the Jews are themselves turning from a narrow view of forgiveness and receiving their own change of heart.

What do the verses below say is God's response to true repentance?

"For if you return to the Lord, your brothers and your sons will find compassion before those who led them captive and will return to this land. For the Lord your God is gracious and compassionate, and will not turn His face away from you if you return to Him." 2 Chronicles 30:9

"Turn to my reproof. Behold, I will pour out my spirit on you; I will make my words known to you." Proverbs 1:23

"And rend your heart and not your garments. Now return to the Lord your God, for He is gracious and compassionate, slow to anger, abounding in loving-kindness and relenting of evil." Joel 2:13

7. Who are the "Gentiles" in your world—those you need to reach out to that you haven't considered before? Prayerfully think about those you have always thought have no interest in hearing the Gospel. In what ways could you reach out to them with the message of hope?

STUDY FOUR | Acts 11:19–12:5
The Gospel Goes to Antioch

Much had been accomplished through the Church by God's Spirit since the death of Stephen: the Samaritans heard the Gospel, an Ethiopian was converted, Saul received Christ, and the Gospel was given to the Gentiles. These newly named Christians were changing the world, and Antioch was the next stop. As Gentiles readily received the Gospel, the Jews remained eager to kill and imprison Christ's followers. Thank God for the men and women who boldly shared the Good News in the midst of great suffering. Centuries and continents apart, we are the fruit of their faithful labor in His name. May God continue to expand His kingdom beyond our earthly expectations.

Empowered: The Amazing Church of Jesus Christ

19 So then those who were scattered because of the persecution that occurred in connection with Stephen made their way to Phoenicia and Cyprus and Antioch, speaking the word to no one except to Jews alone. **20** But there were some of them, men of Cyprus and Cyrene, who came to Antioch and began speaking to the Greeks also, preaching the Lord Jesus. **21** And the hand of the Lord was with them, and a large number who believed turned to the Lord. **22** The news about them reached the ears of the church at Jerusalem, and they sent Barnabas off to Antioch. **23** Then when he arrived and witnessed the grace of God, he rejoiced and began to encourage them all with resolute heart to remain true to the Lord;**24** for he was a good man, and full of the Holy Spirit and of faith. And considerable numbers were brought to the Lord. **25** And he left for Tarsus to look for Saul; **26** and when he had found him, he brought him to Antioch. And for an entire year they met with the church and taught considerable numbers; and the disciples were first called Christians in Antioch.

27 Now at this time some prophets came down from Jerusalem to Antioch. **28** One of them named Agabus stood up and began to indicate by the Spirit that there would certainly be a great famine all over the world. And this took place in the reign of Claudius. **29** And in the proportion that any of the disciples had means, each of them determined to send a contribution for the relief of the brethren living in Judea. **30** And this they did, sending it in charge of Barnabas and Saul to the elders.

12 Now about that time Herod the king laid hands on some who belonged to the church in order to mistreat them. **2** And he had James the brother of John put to death with a sword. **3** When he saw that it pleased the Jews, he proceeded to arrest Peter also. Now it was during the days of Unleavened Bread. **4** When he had seized him, he put him in prison, delivering him to four squads of soldiers to guard him, intending after the Passover to bring him out before the people. **5** So Peter was kept in the prison, but prayer for him was being made fervently by the church to God.

1. Where did the scattered believers go in verse 19 and how did they limit their teaching?

2. "But" signifies a change of direction or contrast. What is the change noted in verse 20?

> The Greek word for "persecution" in verse 19 means to crush, press together, squeeze in. It conveys the idea of being placed under pressure or crushed by a weight. In other words, these were not light inconveniences. The persecution of the Church was intensifying.

3. What evidence in verse 21 reveals their action pleased the Lord?

Antioch was 300 miles north of Jerusalem with a population of more than half a million people. It was the third largest Roman city at the time and a major commerce hub. Because of its proximity to pagan temples, Antioch was known for its moral laxity. (Refer to map on page 84 for location.)

4. Verse 23 records the wise advice Barnabas gave the new believers. What was it? What does that say to you about the kind of encouragement we should offer one another?

5. Verse 24 reinforces the character references we've already been given about Barnabas (Acts 4:36, 9:27) and his reputation. Who has God placed as a Barnabas in your life? In what way have you served as a Barnabas for someone else?

6. After seeing the church in Antioch, Barnabas recognizes this body of Christ needs teaching and guidance as it continues to grow. Who does the Holy Spirit bring to Barnabas' mind to help and what is the outcome of their ministry together? (Acts 11:25–26)

It was no compliment that the disciples were called "Christians" by the citizens of Antioch. Loosely translated, "Christian" means "Christ's ones" or "Jesus people." Based on the mixture of languages used in crafting this word, scholars agree this was a slang term and used in a derogatory manner to describe those who lived in a way that reflected the teachings of their Master.

7. Visible evidence of the grace of God is first mentioned in verse 23. What is continual evidence of God's grace in action seen in the disciples in Antioch in verse 29?

8. What do we learn about the relationship between the Jews and the Christian church at this time? (vv. 3–4)

9. How did the church respond to Peter's arrest? (v. 5)

The word "fervently" here means unceasing activity that involves a degree of intensity and perseverance. In the Greek, it's the idea of straining a muscle to the limit.

Empowered: The Amazing Church of Jesus Christ

10. King Herod had his position of power and popularity among the people on his side. The Christians had prayer—"Therefore let us draw near with confidence to the throne of grace, so that we may receive mercy and find grace to help in time of need." (Hebrews 4:16)

Which "throne" is more effective?

A DEEPER LOOK

According to Acts 11:19, Stephen's life—even in death—is still having an impact on the kingdom of God. How has God used pain in your life to bring glory to His name and helped you share the gift of eternal life with others? In what way has suffering opened your eyes to see the lost in need of hope around you?

STUDY FIVE | Acts 12:6–25 | A Miraculous Escape

Heavily bound and guarded, Peter was prepared to die. The king was on a tirade, obsessed with the praises of men. James had just been brutally murdered; there was no reason to believe Peter would be spared. That's why his rescue seemed so preposterous. The Church had been praying, but perhaps just for peace and comfort—not for actual release. The knock at the door was written off as wishful thinking, until his friends saw Peter face to face. His deliverance meant death for the jailers and disappointment for the Jews. And Herod—the worst offender of the glory of God—would die riddled with worms, a far fall for this self-exalting ruler. Yet the hope of Christ continued to spread, giving Saul unbounded opportunity to tell the story of the Light that opened his eyes.

---

6 On the very night when Herod was about to bring him forward, Peter was sleeping between two soldiers, bound with two chains, and guards in front of the door were watching over the prison. **7** And behold, an angel of the Lord suddenly appeared and a light shone in the cell; and he struck Peter's side and woke him up, saying, "Get up quickly." And his chains fell off his hands. **8** And the angel said to him, "Gird yourself and put on your sandals." And he did so. And he said to him, "Wrap your cloak around you and follow me." **9** And he went out and continued to follow, and he did not know that what was being done by the angel was real, but thought he was seeing a vision. **10** When they had passed the first and second guard, they came to the iron gate that leads into the city, which opened for them by itself; and they went out and went along one street, and immediately the angel departed from him. **11** When Peter came to himself, he said, "Now I know for sure that the Lord has sent forth His angel and rescued me from the hand of Herod and from all that the Jewish people were expecting." **12** And when he realized this, he went to the house of Mary, the mother of John who was also called Mark, where many were gathered together and were praying. **13** When he knocked at the door of the gate, a servant-girl named Rhoda came to answer. **14** When she recognized Peter's voice, because of her joy she did not open the gate, but ran in and announced that Peter was standing in front of the gate. **15** They said to her, "You are out of your mind!" But she kept insisting that it was so. They kept saying, "It is his angel." **16** But Peter continued knocking; and when they had opened the door, they saw him and were amazed. **17** But motioning to them with his hand to be silent, he described to them how the Lord had led him out of the prison. And he said, "Report these things to James and the brethren." Then he left and went to another place.

18 Now when day came, there was no small disturbance among the soldiers as to what could have become of Peter. **19** When Herod had searched for him and had not found him, he examined the guards and ordered that they be led away to execution. Then he went down from Judea to Caesarea and was spending time there.

20 Now he was very angry with the people of Tyre and Sidon; and with one accord they came to him, and having won over Blastus the king's chamberlain, they were asking for peace, because their country was fed by the king's country. **21** On an appointed day Herod, having put on his royal apparel, took his seat on the rostrum and began delivering an address to them. **22** The people kept crying out, "The voice of a god and not of a man!" **23** And immediately an angel of the Lord struck him because he did not give God the glory, and he was eaten by worms and died.

24 But the word of the Lord continued to grow and to be multiplied.

25 And Barnabas and Saul returned from Jerusalem when they had fulfilled their mission, taking along with them John, who was also called Mark.

---

1. The Lord sent an angel to rescue Peter just hours before he would be called to stand before Herod. What were the angel's instructions in Acts 12:7–9? How were Peter's barriers to freedom supernaturally overcome? (vv. 7, 10)

2. What was going through Peter's mind according to verse 9?

3. God could have rescued Peter at any point during the eight days he sat in prison. How do you respond when God doesn't answer your prayer when or how you think He should? Do you trust Him even if He doesn't follow your lead?

4. What do you think this delay could have taught the Church? What have His "delays" taught you?

5. What evidence is there in this passage that the church was praying without completely believing God would answer? (vv. 15–16)

6. What is the difference between believing that "God can" and "God will?" What does praying God's will look like in your life?

7. What happened as a result of Peter's escape? What was taking place in Caesarea between the people and their king? (vv. 19–20)

> Tyre and Sidon were large commercial cities on the coast and received large amounts of grain and fruits from Judea. Herod had cut off their supplies, which stirred the two cities to action.

8. In verse 21, King Herod sits on the city's judgment seat (rostrum) in his royal dress, which is described by the ancient historian Josephus as made of silver that reflected the sun so as to be nearly impossible to look at: "so resplendent as to spread a horror over those that looked intently upon him."

   How did the people respond to Herod in verse 22?

9. Based on verse 23, why did the angel strike Herod?

10. What does Herod's death communicate about the importance of giving God the glory in all things? How do these verses attest to this truth?

   Isaiah 42:8

Isaiah 48:9–11

Ezekiel 36:23

Romans 11:36

A DEEPER LOOK

Read Isaiah 55:10–11. It provides ideal commentary on the state of the Gospel in Acts 12:24. What is being accomplished in spite of intense and intentional persecution of the Church and God's people?

Week 6 Teaching Notes

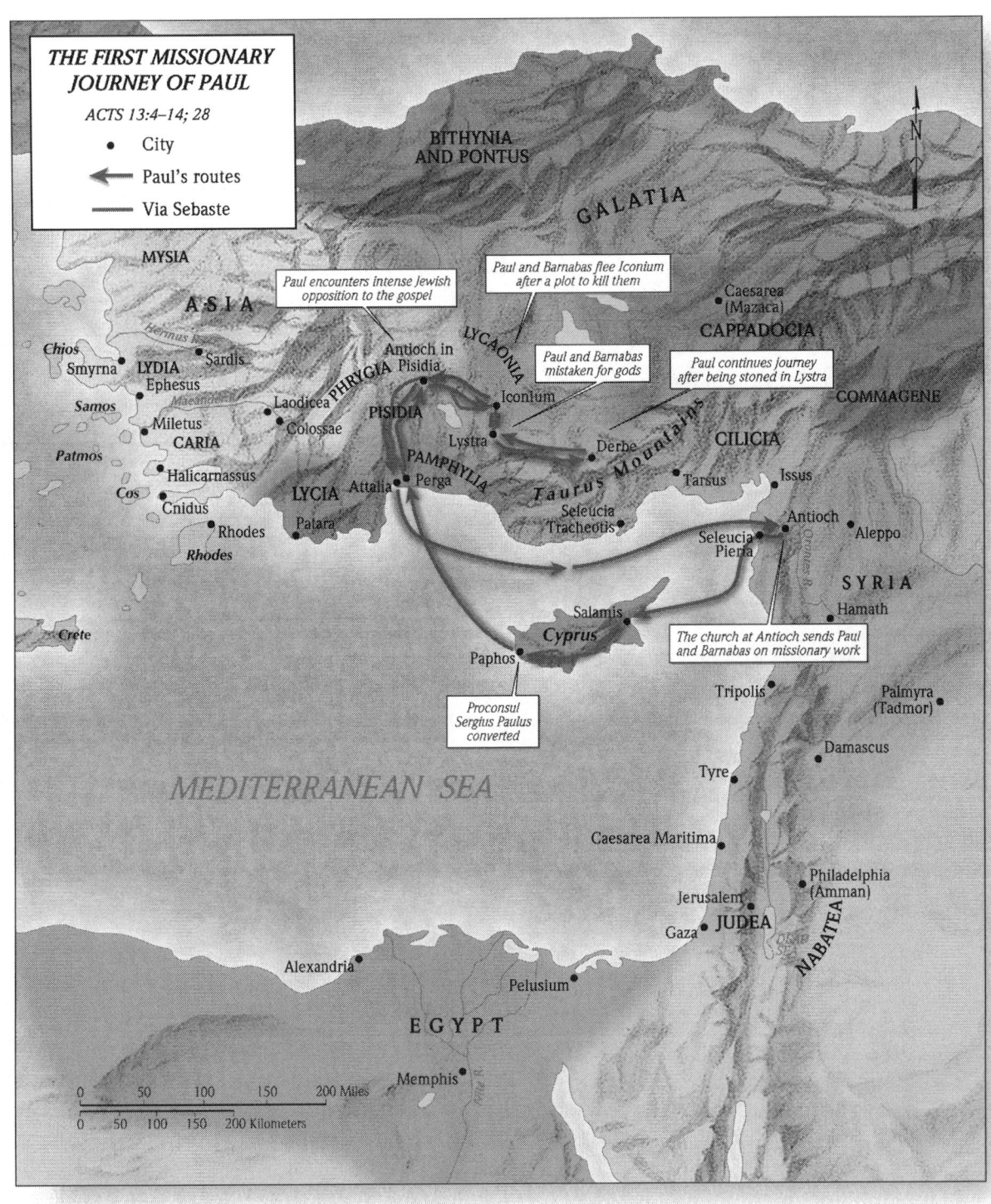

THE FIRST MISSIONARY
JOURNEY OF PAUL

ACTS 13:4–14; 28

- • City
- ← Paul's routes
- — Via Sebaste

BITHYNIA AND PONTUS

GALATIA

MYSIA

ASIA

Paul encounters intense Jewish
opposition to the gospel

Paul and Barnabas flee Iconium
after a plot to kill them

Caesarea
(Mazaca)

CAPPADOCIA

Chios

Smyrna

LYDIA

Sardis

Ephesus

Antioch in
Pisidia

PHRYGIA

LYCAONIA

Paul and Barnabas
mistaken for gods

Iconium

Paul continues journey
after being stoned in Lystra

COMMAGENE

Laodicea

Samos

Miletus

Colossae

PISIDIA

Lystra

Derbe

CILICIA

CARIA

Patmos

Halicarnassus

PAMPHYLIA

Taurus Mountains

Tarsus

Issus

Cos

Cnidus

LYCIA

Attalia

Perga

Seleucia
Tracheotis

Antioch

Aleppo

Rhodes

Patara

Seleucia
Pieria

SYRIA

Rhodes

Hamath

Crete

Salamis

Cyprus

The church at Antioch sends Paul
and Barnabas on missionary work

Paphos

Proconsul
Sergius Paulus
converted

Tripolis

Palmyra
(Tadmor)

MEDITERRANEAN SEA

Damascus

Tyre

Caesarea Maritima

Philadelphia
(Amman)

Jerusalem

Gaza

JUDEA

NABATEA

Alexandria

Pelusium

EGYPT

0   50   100   150   200 Miles
0   50   100   150   200 Kilometers

Memphis

Acts 13–14

The First Missionary Journey

Time spent in the presence of the Lord can prepare your heart for anything. In this case, it was a call to share and suffer for the sake of the Gospel. Equipped by the Holy Spirit, Barnabas and Saul humbly submitted to God's call to go. And the Church eagerly sent them out with joy.

They could not have anticipated the people and circumstances they encountered: healing miracles and false prophets, open doors and fierce opposition, growing believers and deep disappointment.

No doubt Paul saw his former self in the hard-hearted Jews he boldly engaged with, but that old man was gone. Paul had been made new. The transition from his Jewish name "Saul" to "Paul"—his Roman name—is marked during this journey. While this change signals an expanded focus in his ministry, his heart would always long for the people of Israel to be saved. (Romans 10:1)

The ups and downs of this two-year mission would cause most to turn back, but these earliest evangelists followed the example of Christ: they ran the race with endurance, daily picking up their cross, for the joy of following in His steps.

KEY VERSE:

"Brethren, sons of Abraham's family, and those among you who fear God, to us the message of this salvation has been sent."

ACTS 13:26

STUDY ONE | Acts 13:1–12
Barnabas and Saul Sent from Antioch

There is no such thing as a "typical worship service" when you're worshipping the God of the universe, but this one was extraordinary. The call to "go" came, and Barnabas and Saul went, beginning their journey that would take them more than 1,200 miles from home and "to the Jew first" every time (Romans 1:16). An interesting encounter with a powerful Roman governor and his personal soothsayer had an unexpected result. Mercy and grace were extended, but only the eyes of one man were opened. This exchange could be considered a foreshadowing for the course of Paul's ministry: the Jews would be blind to the truth, but the Gentiles would clearly see.

¹ Now there were at Antioch, in the church that was there, prophets and teachers: Barnabas, and Simeon who was called Niger, and Lucius of Cyrene, and Manaen who had been brought up with Herod the tetrarch, and Saul. ² While they were ministering to the Lord and fasting, the Holy Spirit said, "Set apart for Me Barnabas and Saul for the work to which I have called them." ³ Then, when they had fasted and prayed and laid their hands on them, they sent them away.

⁴ So, being sent out by the Holy Spirit, they went down to Seleucia and from there they sailed to Cyprus. ⁵ When they reached Salamis, they began to proclaim the word of God in the synagogues of the Jews; and they also had John as their helper. ⁶ When they had gone through the whole island as far as Paphos, they found a magician, a Jewish false prophet whose name was Bar-Jesus, ⁷ who was with the proconsul, Sergius Paulus, a man of intelligence. This man summoned Barnabas and Saul and sought to hear the word of God. ⁸ But Elymas the magician (for so his name is translated) was opposing them, seeking to turn the proconsul away from the faith. ⁹ But Saul, who was also known as Paul, filled with the Holy Spirit, fixed his gaze on him, ¹⁰ and said, "You who are full of all deceit and fraud, you son of the devil, you enemy of all righteousness, will you not cease to make crooked the straight ways of the Lord? ¹¹ Now, behold, the hand of the Lord is upon you, and you will be blind and not see the sun for a time." And immediately a mist and a darkness fell upon him, and he went about seeking those who would lead him by the hand. ¹² Then the proconsul believed when he saw what had happened, being amazed at the teaching of the Lord.

The names of the prophets and teachers in verse 1 are Greek. Scholars conclude that Simeon—as well as Lucius—were from North Africa because "Niger" refers to a dark complexion. Herod the tetrarch is also known as Herod Antipas (4 B.C.–39 A.D.). He had John the Baptist imprisoned and killed and also played a role in the crucifixion of Jesus. Scholars say Manaen grew up either as a close childhood friend or "foster brother" in the court. These names and their backgrounds suggest this was a diverse church in every way.

Other Bible translations of this verse use "worship" as another word for "ministering to the Lord."

1. If all you had were verses 1–3 to describe the ministry of the Church, what would you say the Church is called to do?

2. The Holy Spirit sent Barnabas and Saul sixty miles away to Cyprus, the hometown of Barnabas. (Acts 4:36) What did they do when they reached their destination? (Acts 13:4–5)

The John mentioned in verse 5 is also known as John Mark. We learn in Colossians 4:10 that he is Barnabas' cousin.

Empowered: The Amazing Church of Jesus Christ

3. In Acts 13:6, Barnabas and Saul were in Paphos, about ninety miles away from their starting place, when they encountered two men. Who were they and how were they described? (vv. 6–7)

The proconsul was considered the governor of the island. He would have been the highest authority there and appointed by Rome

4. What was Bar-Jesus—called Elymas the magician here—hoping to do in verse 8?

5. What are common ways people are deceived in today's culture? How do the verses below teach us to guard against deception?

"My son, do not forget my teaching, but let your heart keep my commandments; for length of days and years of life and peace they will add to you. Do not let kindness and truth leave you; bind them around your neck, write them on the tablet of your heart. So you will find favor and good repute in the sight of God and man. Trust in the Lord with all your heart and do not lean on your own understanding. In all your ways acknowledge Him, and He will make your paths straight." Proverbs 3:1–6

"And do not be conformed to this world, but be transformed by the renewing of your mind, so that you may prove what the will of God is, that which is good and acceptable and perfect." Romans 12:2

"See to it that no one takes you captive through philosophy and empty deception, according to the tradition of men, according to the elementary principles of the world, rather than according to Christ." Colossians 2:8

"But solid food is for the mature, who because of practice have their senses trained to discern good and evil." Hebrews 5:14

"Beloved, do not believe every spirit, but test the spirits to see whether they are from God, because many false prophets have gone out into the world." 1 John 4:1

6. Acts 13:9 makes a point of telling us that Paul (the Roman version of his Jewish name, Saul) was "filled with the Holy Spirit." He then delivered a strong indictment against Bar-Jesus. What does Paul say Bar-Jesus was full of? (v. 10)

The name Bar-Jesus means "Son of Jesus/Joshua." Paul called him an "enemy of righteousness" then delivered a warning designed to point back to Jesus. What is the warning?

7. Acts 13:11 has been called a "judgment miracle." What happened to Bar-Jesus?

8. How were Sergius Paulus' eyes opened by the blindness of Bar-Jesus? (v. 12)

 9. How has the Word of God helped "open" your eyes?

A DEEPER LOOK

The word "proclaim" means to declare something considered important with due emphasis, sometimes publicly. Acts uses this word nearly every time the Gospel is being shared. It can be tempting to make the truth of the Gospel more "palatable" or at least inoffensive. The Bible never shrinks back from the laser focus of God's message to the world, regardless of the situation or circumstance.

Determine the focus of what is being proclaimed in the verses below.

Acts 4:2

1 Corinthians 2:1–5

Colossians 1:28

Whether it's a public platform or a private meeting, what should be our focus when we proclaim the Gospel to others? How can you ensure what you say about Jesus and His offer of life is clear, complete, and true?

STUDY TWO | Acts 13:13–25
Paul Preaches at Pisidian Antioch

When Paul is given an open invitation to speak, don't expect ear tickling—be prepared for soul-searing, heart-moving truth! Paul wisely identifies with his hearers in this Sabbath setting, recounting their common history and testifying to the goodness and faithfulness of their God through it all. Paul then takes full advantage of his opportunity and makes sure these religious men recognize what every event in their collective past is pointing to: the Messiah Jesus, the promised fulfillment they had all been waiting for.

---

13 Now Paul and his companions put out to sea from Paphos and came to Perga in Pamphylia; but John left them and returned to Jerusalem. **14** But going on from Perga, they arrived at Pisidian Antioch, and on the Sabbath day they went into the synagogue and sat down. **15** After the reading of the Law and the Prophets the synagogue officials sent to them, saying, "Brethren, if you have any word of exhortation for the people, say it." **16** Paul stood up, and motioning with his hand said,

"Men of Israel, and you who fear God, listen: **17** The God of this people Israel chose our fathers and made the people great during their stay in the land of Egypt, and with an uplifted arm He led them out from it. **18** For a period of about forty years He put up with them in the wilderness. **19** When He had destroyed seven nations in the land of Canaan, He distributed their land as an inheritance—all of which took about four hundred and fifty years. **20** After these things He gave them judges until Samuel the prophet. **21** Then they asked for a king, and God gave them Saul the son of Kish, a man of the tribe of Benjamin, for forty years. **22** After He had removed him, He raised up David to be their king, concerning whom He also testified and said, 'I have found David the son of Jesse, a man after My heart, who will do all My will.' **23** From the descendants of this man, according to promise, God has brought to Israel a Savior, Jesus, **24** after John had proclaimed before His coming a baptism of repentance to all the people of Israel. **25** And while John was completing his course, he kept saying, 'What do you suppose that I am? I am not He. But behold, one is coming after me the sandals of whose feet I am not worthy to untie.'

---

1. Paul and his team travel more than 112 miles in verse 13. What notable shift in manpower takes place after they arrive in Perga?

2. What encouragement and instruction do the scriptures below provide for times of disappointment?

"I sought the Lord, and He answered me, and delivered me from all my fears ... The angel of the Lord encamps around those who fear Him, and rescues them. O taste and see that the Lord is good; how blessed is the man who takes refuge in Him!" Psalm 34:4,7–8

"I waited patiently for the Lord; and He inclined to me and heard my cry." Psalm 40:1

"Trust in Him at all times, O people; pour out your heart before Him; God is a refuge for us." Psalm 62:8

"Yet those who wait for the Lord will gain new strength; they will mount up with wings like eagles, they will run and not get tired, they will walk and not become weary." Isaiah 40:31

"And not only this, but we also exult in our tribulations, knowing that tribulation brings about perseverance; and perseverance, proven character; and proven character, hope; and hope does not disappoint, because the love of God has been poured out within our hearts through the Holy Spirit who was given to us." Romans 5:3–5

"But in all these things we overwhelmingly conquer through Him who loved us. For I am convinced that neither death, nor life, nor angels, nor principalities, nor things present, nor things to come, nor powers, nor height, nor depth, nor any other created thing, will be able to separate us from the love of God, which is in Christ Jesus our Lord." Romans 8:37–39

> Pisidian Antioch stood on a plateau 3,600 feet above sea level. To get there, Paul and Barnabas would have crossed a range of mountains on one of the most physically challenging roads in the region. The road was also notorious for robbers.

3. Paul was invited to speak by the synagogue officials. Who did he address his remarks to in Acts 13:16?

4. Paul wisely considers his setting and audience and begins his sermon with truths from their common history.

Read verses 17–22. In the chart on the next page, list all the things God did in these verses for the children of Israel. Then list the attribute(s) of God (merciful, powerful, holy, loving) that is reflected in His actions (see example).

Empowered: The Amazing Church of Jesus Christ

VERSE	WHAT GOD DID	WHO GOD IS
Acts 13:17	God chose Israel to be His people	Sovereign
Acts 13:18		
Acts 13:19		
Acts 13:20		
Acts 13:21		
Acts 13:22		

5. Paul then jumped over 1,000 years of history in verse 23 and spoke of a promise fulfilled. What is that promise? (see 2 Samuel 7:12–17, Jeremiah 23:5–6)

6. How did Paul say John had prepared the people for the coming of the Messiah? (Acts 13:24–25)

7. This first portion of Paul's sermon—the longest one of his in Acts—is the story of God's people, the nation He chose, not "because you were more in number than any of the peoples, for you were the fewest of all peoples, but because the Lord loved you and kept the oath which He swore to your forefathers..." (Deuteronomy 7:7b–8a)

God is the one who chose you—not because of anything you did or have done, but by His grace. What is your salvation story?

8. How has God used the people, places, and events of your life to draw you to Himself?

In what ways has He blessed you, over time, with a deeper desire and capacity to love and know Him more?

STUDY THREE | Acts 13:26–43
A Longing to Hear More

In the past, Paul said, familiarity bred contempt. The Jews' regular reading of the "utterances of the prophets" fell like seeds in a wasteland. They knew the signs to look for but, with eyes unwilling to see, the Jews had rejected their Messiah. Paul used King David and sacred poetry to encourage his listeners that all was not lost; the offer of freedom and forgiveness remains. The Holy Spirit awakened hope in God's people, and they could not wait to hear more.

---

26 "Brethren, sons of Abraham's family, and those among you who fear God, to us the message of this salvation has been sent. 27 For those who live in Jerusalem, and their rulers, recognizing neither Him nor the utterances of the prophets which are read every Sabbath, fulfilled these by condemning Him. 28 And though they found no ground for putting Him to death, they asked Pilate that He be executed. 29 When they had carried out all that was written concerning Him, they took Him down from the cross and laid Him in a tomb. 30 But God raised Him from the dead; 31 and for many days He appeared to those who came up with Him from Galilee to Jerusalem, the very ones who are now His witnesses to the people. 32 And we preach to you the good news of the promise made to the fathers, 33 that God has fulfilled this promise to our children in that He raised up Jesus, as it is also written in the second Psalm, 'You are My Son; today I have begotten You.' 34 As for the fact that He raised Him up from the dead, no longer to return to decay, He has spoken in this way: 'I will give you the holy and sure blessings of David.' 35 Therefore He also says in another Psalm, 'You will not allow Your Holy One to undergo decay.' 36 For David, after he had served the purpose of God in his own generation,

Empowered: The Amazing Church of Jesus Christ

fell asleep, and was laid among his fathers and underwent decay; **37** but He whom God raised did not undergo decay. **38** Therefore let it be known to you, brethren, that through Him forgiveness of sins is proclaimed to you, **39** and through Him everyone who believes is freed from all things, from which you could not be freed through the Law of Moses. **40** Therefore take heed, so that the thing spoken of in the Prophets may not come upon you:

41 'Behold, you scoffers, and marvel, and perish;
For I am accomplishing a work in your days,
A work which you will never believe, though someone should describe it to you.'"

42 As Paul and Barnabas were going out, the people kept begging that these things might be spoken to them the next Sabbath. **43** Now when the meeting of the synagogue had broken up, many of the Jews and of the God-fearing proselytes followed Paul and Barnabas, who, speaking to them, were urging them to continue in the grace of God.

---

1. How did Paul connect to his hearers and offer good news in verse 26?

2. What irony did Paul point out about the Jews and their understanding of Scripture in Acts 13:27–28?

3. How do Acts 13:30–31 provide assurance that what Paul is testifying about is true?

4. What "good news" was Paul preaching at that moment? (vv. 32–33)

5. How do Paul and Scripture say David and Jesus are different; and why is that important? (vv. 35–37)

6. There are two "through Him" statements in verses 38–39. What does Paul say is provided to the people then and to us today "through Him?"

    1.

    2.

7. Paul gives a call for accountability to his hearers at the end of his sermon. What does he warn them—and us—about in verses 40–41?

8. Choose at least ONE of the verses below and determine what Scripture teaches us about the sins we are unable to see and how we are called to respond to the Spirit's work in our hearts.

    Psalm 19:12–14   Romans 2:1–3
    Psalm 139:23–24   1 John 1:8–10
    Matthew 7:1–5   Revelation 3:17–19
    Luke 11:33–36

9. Have you ever wrestled with a spiritual "blind spot," unaware of or unable to see the ways God wants to work in your life?

A DEEPER LOOK

Read Titus 2:11–14. We know the grace of God saves us, but how does God's grace teach us as well?

How does this passage help you understand what it means to follow the words of Paul and Barnabas and "continue in the grace of God?" (Acts 13:43)

Empowered: The Amazing Church of Jesus Christ

STUDY FOUR | Acts 13:44–14:7
Acceptance and Opposition

We can safely assume that Paul and Barnabas continued their dialogue with the Jews at Pisidian Antioch because, one week later, nearly everyone in the city showed up for Paul's "part two." Among them were those eager to cast stones—figuratively and literally. These are the kind of hearts even hope and light won't penetrate, and Paul knew it was time for the message to move on. The Gentiles emerged among the chosen, causing much rejoicing in the midst of great trials. As the mission team pressed forward, trouble continued to follow. Division arose but, under the protective hand of God and by the power of the Holy Spirit, Paul and Barnabas persevered, determined to bring salvation to the end of the earth.

---

44 The next Sabbath nearly the whole city assembled to hear the word of the Lord. 45 But when the Jews saw the crowds, they were filled with jealousy and began contradicting the things spoken by Paul, and were blaspheming. 46 Paul and Barnabas spoke out boldly and said, "It was necessary that the word of God be spoken to you first; since you repudiate it and judge yourselves unworthy of eternal life, behold, we are turning to the Gentiles. 47 For so the Lord has commanded us,

'I have placed You as a light for the Gentiles,
That You may bring salvation to the end of the earth.'"

48 When the Gentiles heard this, they began rejoicing and glorifying the word of the Lord; and as many as had been appointed to eternal life believed. 49 And the word of the Lord was being spread through the whole region. 50 But the Jews incited the devout women of prominence and the leading men of the city, and instigated a persecution against Paul and Barnabas, and drove them out of their district. 51 But they shook off the dust of their feet in protest against them and went to Iconium. 52 And the disciples were continually filled with joy and with the Holy Spirit.

14 1 In Iconium they entered the synagogue of the Jews together, and spoke in such a manner that a large number of people believed, both of Jews and of Greeks. 2 But the Jews who disbelieved stirred up the minds of the Gentiles and embittered them against the brethren. 3 Therefore they spent a long time there speaking boldly with reliance upon the Lord, who was testifying to the word of His grace, granting that signs and wonders be done by their hands. 4 But the people of the city were divided; and some sided with the Jews, and some with the apostles. 5 And when an attempt was made by both the Gentiles and the Jews with their rulers, to mistreat and to stone them, 6 they became aware of it and fled to the cities of Lycaonia, Lystra and Derbe, and the surrounding region; 7 and there they continued to preach the gospel.

---

1. One week later, the word of the Lord through Paul was still having its effect. How do we know this? (v. 44) How did the Jews respond to this turnout? (v. 45)

2. Acts 13:46 is a significant turning point in the ministry of Paul and the proclamation of the Gospel. What is it?

3. Paul made a proclamation in Acts 13:46–47. How did the Gentiles respond to it? (v. 48)

What evidence do we see in verse 49 that these Gentile converts embraced Jesus' commands seen in Matthew 28:16–20?

4. "But the Jews" has become a familiar phrase in Acts thus far. What did they decide to do about the spread of the Word of the Lord? (Acts 13:50)

5. In Acts 13:51 how did Paul and Barnabas follow Jesus' instruction given in Luke 10:10–12, 16?

6. How is the disciples' attitude in verse 52 a picture of 1 Peter 1:6–8?

7. The location changes in Acts 14:1 but not the pattern. Where did Paul and Barnabas go when they reached Iconium? What was the result? What opposition did they encounter? (vv. 1–2)

8. What were Paul and Barnabus relying on the Lord to do? (v. 3)

9. The division turned violent, and Paul and Barnabas needed to respond. (vv. 5–6) How do Jesus' words in Matthew 10:16, 23 speak to their decision?

10. What is it about the message of the Gospel that makes it divisive (and offensive) to some, then and now?

A DEEPER LOOK

Look back on verse 52 and meditate for a moment on the reality of the situation for the new disciples in Pisidian Antioch. They had just witnessed the intentional persecution Paul and Barnabas endured because of their faith. And yet they were continually "_____ _____ _____and _____ _____ _____ _____."

These new believers were promised that same persecution—not simply inconvenienced by the "flat tires" of life, but crushed and squeezed like a grape in a winepress. These trials would come to them from within their own community, at the hands of former friends and neighbors. And yet these disciples are forever preserved in God's Word as being filled with joy.

How is it possible that they rejoiced in the face of rejection and hardship?

What hope and encouragement do 1 Peter 4:12–14 and James 1:2–4 offer this situation?

What hope and encouragement do you find in God's words to you today?

At Lystra, Paul and Barnabas demonstrated they cared more for the name of Jesus than their own safety. The pair rejected the offer to be honored as gods, yet embraced the chance to suffer more than once for their Savior. And what stories they had to share when they returned home! This would be Paul's shortest missionary journey. Depending on how you calculate it, Paul and Barnabas traveled anywhere from 1,200 to 1,500 miles together over two years. But the Spirit's impact through these willing vessels is incalculable. Only in heaven will we know how many walked through the door of faith because of their obedience and sacrifice in Jesus' name.

---

8 At Lystra a man was sitting who had no strength in his feet, lame from his mother's womb, who had never walked. **9** This man was listening to Paul as he spoke, who, when he had fixed his gaze on him and had seen that he had faith to be made well, **10** said with a loud voice, "Stand upright on your feet." And he leaped up and began to walk. **11** When the crowds saw what Paul had done, they raised their voice, saying in the Lycaonian language, "The gods have become like men and have come down to us." **12** And they began calling Barnabas, Zeus, and Paul, Hermes, because he was the chief speaker. **13** The priest of Zeus, whose temple was just outside the city, brought oxen and garlands to the gates, and wanted to offer sacrifice with the crowds. **14** But when the apostles Barnabas and Paul heard of it, they tore their robes and rushed out into the crowd, crying out **15** and saying, "Men, why are you doing these things? We are also men of the same nature as you, and preach the gospel to you that you should turn from these vain things to a living God, who made the heaven and the earth and the sea and all that is in them. **16** In the generations gone by He permitted all the nations to go their own ways; **17** and yet He did not leave Himself without witness, in that He did good and gave you rains from heaven and fruitful seasons, satisfying your hearts with food and gladness." **18** Even saying these things, with difficulty they restrained the crowds from offering sacrifice to them.

19 But Jews came from Antioch and Iconium, and having won over the crowds, they stoned Paul and dragged him out of the city, supposing him to be dead. **20** But while the disciples stood around him, he got up and entered the city. The next day he went away with Barnabas to Derbe. **21** After they had preached the gospel to that city and had made many disciples, they returned to Lystra and to Iconium and to Antioch, **22** strengthening the souls of the disciples, encouraging them to continue in the faith, and saying, "Through many tribulations we must enter the kingdom of God." **23** When they had appointed elders for them in every church, having prayed with fasting, they commended them to the Lord in whom they had believed.

24 They passed through Pisidia and came into Pamphylia. **25** When they had spoken the word in Perga, they went down to Attalia. **26** From there they sailed to Antioch, from which they had been commended to the grace of God for the work that they had accomplished. **27** When they had arrived and gathered the church together, they began to report all things that God had done with them and how He had opened a door of faith to the Gentiles. **28** And they spent a long time with the disciples.

---

1. Paul and Barnabas encountered a man in Lystra. How did Dr. Luke describe him and what insight did the Holy Spirit give Paul regarding him? (vv.8–9)

2. How did the people respond to the miraculous healings in Acts 14:11–13?

3. What, according to Scripture, are the dangers of idolatry? Choose at least ONE of the verses below and record your observations.

   Deuteronomy 7:25   Psalm 135:15–18
   Judges 10:13–14   Isaiah 45:20
   Psalm 16:4   Jonah 2:8

4. What and who are common idols in today's culture? What idolatrous tendencies compete in your heart for the adoration of God?

5. How do the gods the people worshipped compare to the one true God, according to verse 15?

6. How did Paul and Barnabas say the Lord had shown His grace to them—and to all people—in the past? (Acts 14:16–17)

7. An angry mob from Antioch and Iconium with unfinished business showed up in Acts 14:19. What did the mob accomplish and do to Paul? What miraculously happened to Paul? (v.20)

8. We see Paul and Barnabus continue to display supernatural courage, returning to the cities where they had experienced extreme persecution. Why did they go? (vv. 19–22)

9. What structure did they put in place in Acts 14:23?

10. What did Paul and Barnabas do upon their arrival back "home" in Acts 14:27? How did Paul and Barnabas describe their ministry experience?

Empowered: The Amazing Church of Jesus Christ

WEEK 7 TEACHING NOTES

Empowered: The Amazing Church of Jesus Christ

Acts 15:1–16:40

The Jerusalem Council and the Church in Macedonia

With only a casual read, Acts 15 might seem like a record of a typical boring church meeting: people discuss, disagree, make a decision, and move on. But the events leading up to (and every day after) the Jerusalem Council were anything but boring. And with the history of God's people in view, the decision they made together is truly breathtaking.

There is also a heartbreaking separation in this chapter, followed by a compelling dream in Acts 16. This moved Paul, with a new set of companions, into his second missionary journey, traveling to a part of the world that wasn't even on his radar. It is in this "far country" that one of the most well-known churches in Scripture is born. And the method was most unexpected.

A woman and her friends worshipping by the riverside and a suicidal jailer were among the first members of this new body of believers. This was the beginning of the church in Europe, and the church in Europe is the beginning of us—modern-day believers who wouldn't have had a chance without the Spirit assembling this unlikely group of open-hearted Philippians and the man who followed God's call at every cost.

KEY VERSE:

"And when Paul had seen the vision, immediately we sought to go on into Macedonia, concluding that God had called us to preach the gospel to them."

Acts 16:10

STUDY ONE | **Acts 15:1–12**
The Decision on Doctrine

If Acts 10 answered the question of "if" with regard to the Gentile's salvation, Acts 15 answered the question "how." Misguided thinking unchecked by truth can lead to legalism—or worse, heresy. A vocal group of Jews with strong ties to the Law had a limited view of grace and wanted to obligate Gentiles to their preferences. The question of the day was: *do Gentiles have to become Jews to become Christians?* For the early Church, this was new territory and worthy of wise discussion. So, with the Holy Spirit as their compass and the Word of God as their road map, a Council convened to weigh the effect of the Law against the merits of grace.

---

1 Some men came down from Judea and began teaching the brethren, "Unless you are circumcised according to the custom of Moses, you cannot be saved." **2** And when Paul and Barnabas had great dissension and debate with them, the brethren determined that Paul and Barnabas and some others of them should go up to Jerusalem to the apostles and elders concerning this issue. **3** Therefore, being sent on their way by the church, they were passing through both Phoenicia and Samaria, describing in detail the conversion of the Gentiles, and were bringing great joy to all the brethren. **4** When they arrived at Jerusalem, they were received by the church and the apostles and the elders, and they reported all that God had done with them. **5** But some of the sect of the Pharisees who had believed stood up, saying, "It is necessary to circumcise them and to direct them to observe the Law of Moses."

6 The apostles and the elders came together to look into this matter. **7** After there had been much debate, Peter stood up and said to them, "Brethren, you know that in the early days God made a choice among you, that by my mouth the Gentiles would hear the word of the gospel and believe. **8** And God, who knows the heart, testified to them giving them the Holy Spirit, just as He also did to us; **9** and He made no distinction between us and them, cleansing their hearts by faith. **10** Now therefore why do you put God to the test by placing upon the neck of the disciples a yoke which neither our fathers nor we have been able to bear? **11** But we believe that we are saved through the grace of the Lord Jesus, in the same way as they also are."

12 All the people kept silent, and they were listening to Barnabas and Paul as they were relating what signs and wonders God had done through them among the Gentiles.

---

1. We see unauthorized and inaccurate teaching being spread among the Gentile believers in Antioch in verse 1. What was this teaching and who did it come from?

2. How did Paul and Barnabas respond to this teaching and what did the church decide to do? (v.2)

> The Greek word for *dissension* here means, "a lack of agreement respecting policy; strife, discord, dispute, contention." The word for *debate* means "the exchange of words for the purpose of disputing; engaging in contentious, controversial questions."

Empowered: The Amazing Church of Jesus Christ

3. Circumcision has been an issue throughout Acts related to the growth of the Church, especially as the Gospel continues to move beyond the nation of Israel. (To better understand its importance to the Jews, read Genesis 17:9–14.)

   A promise made by God is recorded in Jeremiah 31:31–34 and was ushered in upon the death and resurrection of Jesus Christ. This sign of God's covenant with His people (circumcision) was replaced by the blood of Christ and is succinctly explained in Ephesians 2:8–9.

   Based on the background from Scripture, why was the teaching from the men of Judea in Acts 15:1 not only in error but also harmful to the faith of the Gentiles?

> Circumcision "was important for the preservation of God's people physically. But it was also a symbol of the need for the heart to be cleansed from sin's deadly disease. The really essential surgery needed to happen on the inside, where God calls for taking away fleshly things that keep the heart from being spiritually devoted to Him and from true faith in Him and His will." from *The MacArthur Study Bible*

4. The leaders of the Church in Jerusalem gathered to debate the issue, likely with zeal on both sides. (vv. 6–7) Then Peter, wise and respected among them, stood to speak.

   What choice did God make, according to Peter, in verse 7?

> This is Peter's last appearance in the book of Acts.

   How did He provide assurance that this was His will and that their salvation was "equal" to the Jews? (vv. 8–9)

   Peter asked a pointed question in verse 10. What is the "yoke" he refers to?

5. How does Scripture describe the law as a "yoke" and why is this yoke unbearable?

   Romans 8:1–4

   Galatians 5:1

6. What is the common ground we all stand on in Acts 15:11?

7. From a noisy debate to complete silence, the testimony of Peter left the room speechless. How did Paul and Barnabas then provide support for Peter's position? (v. 12)

A DEEPER LOOK

Using a dictionary, look up the words *legalism* and *heresy* and write the definitions below.

Legalism:

Heresy:

What is the difference between legalism and heresy?

What do they have in common?

What is the example of legalism in Matthew 12:9−14? (see Exodus 20:8−11 for background)

What is the warning against legalism in Colossians 2:20−23?

What is the example of heresy in 1 John 2:22−23?

How does 1 John 4:1−6 teach us how to recognize heresy?

Empowered: The Amazing Church of Jesus Christ

Dissension in the family of God can be so painful, but it is also instructive. And this scene shows us a healthy exchange between brothers in Christ who chose to bend rather than "win." We also see here that the Church was not built by a dictator—one man deciding the doctrine and details. This was Spirit-appointed leadership settling important theological issues, based on the words and life of Jesus Himself. These men knew they must refrain from passing on the burden of the Law. They knew unity would only come from pursuing whatever might lead to peace and mutual building up of the body of Christ. (Romans 14:19)

---

13 After they had stopped speaking, James answered, saying, "Brethren, listen to me.**14** Simeon has related how God first concerned Himself about taking from among the Gentiles a people for His name. **15** With this the words of the Prophets agree, just as it is written,

16 'After these things I will return,
And I will rebuild the tabernacle of David which has fallen,
And I will rebuild its ruins,
And I will restore it,
17 So that the rest of mankind may seek the Lord,
And all the Gentiles who are called by My name,'
18 Says the Lord, who makes these things known from long ago.

19 Therefore it is my judgment that we do not trouble those who are turning to God from among the Gentiles, **20** but that we write to them that they abstain from things contaminated by idols and from fornication and from what is strangled and from blood. **21** For Moses from ancient generations has in every city those who preach him, since he is read in the synagogues every Sabbath."

22 Then it seemed good to the apostles and the elders, with the whole church, to choose men from among them to send to Antioch with Paul and Barnabas—Judas called Barsabbas, and Silas, leading men among the brethren, **23** and they [l]sent this letter by them,

"The apostles and the brethren who are elders, to the brethren in Antioch and Syria and Cilicia who are from the Gentiles, greetings.

24 "Since we have heard that some of our number to whom we gave no instruction have disturbed you with their words, unsettling your souls, **25** it seemed good to us, having become of one mind, to select men to send to you with our beloved Barnabas and Paul,**26** men who have risked their lives for the name of our Lord Jesus Christ. **27** "Therefore we have sent Judas and Silas, who themselves will also report the same things by word of mouth. **28** "For it seemed good to the Holy Spirit and to us to lay upon you no greater burden than these essentials: **29** that you abstain from things sacrificed to idols and from blood and from things strangled and from fornication; if you keep yourselves free from such things, you will do well. Farewell."

1. After Paul and Barnabas finished speaking in verses 13–14, James—another Church leader— added his affirmation to the proceedings. James quoted the prophet Amos, demonstrating his knowledge of and Spirit-given insight into Scripture. (vv. 13–18)

   What does Amos 9:11–12 say God will do and why? (Acts 15:16–17)

2. James stated that, over the centuries, the Prophets all agreed with the truth quoted in Acts 15:16– 18. Read the passages below. What revelation do these prophets affirm about the Gentile nations and God's plan regarding the salvation of the Gentiles?

   Isaiah 2:2

   Zechariah 2:11

   Isaiah 45:21

3. What did James decide they should not do in Acts 15:19?

4. Instead of circumcision, what four things did James want the letter to focus on? (v. 20)

5. The principle behind this is: don't dismiss or disregard the convictions of another. How do the verses below instruct us further on this matter?

   "But take care that this liberty of yours does not somehow become a stumbling block to the weak. For if someone sees you, who have knowledge, dining in an idol's temple, will not his conscience, if he is weak, be strengthened to eat things sacrificed to idols? For through your knowledge he who is weak is ruined, the brother for whose sake Christ died. And so, by sinning against the brethren and wounding their conscience when it is weak, you sin against Christ. Therefore, if food causes my brother to stumble, I will never eat meat again, so that I will not cause my brother to stumble." 1 Corinthians 8:9–13

Empowered: The Amazing Church of Jesus Christ

"… we endure all things so that we will cause no hindrance to the gospel of Christ."
1 Corinthians 9:12b

6. In the opening statement of their letter, the apostles and elders immediately distanced themselves from the wrong teaching that was being dispersed to the new believers. (v. 24) How did they go on to describe the result of the men of Judea's teaching to the congregation?

7. According to Scripture, how can we recognize false teachers? Choose at least ONE of the verses below and decide the biblical response to this experience.

Romans 16:17–18   Titus 1:10–11
2 Timothy 2:16–18

8. What is another expression of the Jerusalem church's unity in this decision and what is the importance of these multiple messengers? (Acts 15:25–27)

9. Based on the events and discussion that took place in Acts 15:1–29, when should we seek compromise or deference with one another in the body of Christ; and when should compromise not be tolerated?

How can you know the difference?

STUDY | **Acts 15:30–16:5**
THREE | **A Sharp Disagreement**

We've seen conflict successfully resolved in the Church; here, we see two friends fail to yield or forgive. We've all been there—choosing our own will over the good of another, sometimes to the detriment of the body of Christ. In the conflict, they were both wrong but, upon inspection, we can understand the intent of their hearts: Paul was focused on the ministry, while Barnabas' priority was the man. So how did God bring good out of a heartbreaking situation? The conflict did not stop the Gospel's spread. In fact, their division multiplied the kingdom of God, proving that—even in human failure—there will always be victory in Christ.

30 So when they were sent away, they went down to Antioch; and having gathered the congregation together, they delivered the letter. **31** When they had read it, they rejoiced because of its encouragement. **32** Judas and Silas, also being prophets themselves, encouraged and strengthened the brethren with a lengthy message. **33** After they had spent time there, they were sent away from the brethren in peace to those who had sent them out.**34** [But it seemed good to Silas to remain there.] **35** But Paul and Barnabas stayed in Antioch, teaching and preaching with many others also, the word of the Lord.

36 After some days Paul said to Barnabas, "Let us return and visit the brethren in every city in which we proclaimed the word of the Lord, and see how they are." **37** Barnabas wanted to take John, called Mark, along with them also. **38** But Paul kept insisting that they should not take him along who had deserted them in Pamphylia and had not gone with them to the work. **39** And there occurred such a sharp disagreement that they separated from one another, and Barnabas took Mark with him and sailed away to Cyprus. **40** But Paul chose Silas and left, being committed by the brethren to the grace of the Lord. **41** And he was traveling through Syria and Cilicia, strengthening the churches.

16 Paul came also to Derbe and to Lystra. And a disciple was there, named Timothy, the son of a Jewish woman who was a believer, but his father was a Greek, **2** and he was well spoken of by the brethren who were in Lystra and Iconium. **3** Paul wanted this man to go with him; and he took him and circumcised him because of the Jews who were in those parts, for they all knew that his father was a Greek. **4** Now while they were passing through the cities, they were delivering the decrees which had been decided upon by the apostles and elders who were in Jerusalem, for them to observe. **5** So the churches were being strengthened in the faith, and were increasing in number daily.

---

1. How did the Antioch believers respond to the letter from Jerusalem in verse 31?

2. In what other ways did the apostles spend their time with their brothers and sisters in Antioch? (vv. 32–35)

3. Paul was an evangelist with a shepherd's heart. What was his specific desire—or purpose—for this next missionary journey? (v. 36)

4. Verses 37–38 reveal a difference of opinion and ministry strategy. What was it? How did Paul characterize Mark's actions in verse 38?

5. We read of a heartbreaking shift in Paul and Barnabas' fifteen-year friendship. What happened? (vv. 39–41)

> "The verb is in the imperfect tense, which means a continual quarrel—an unending, unyielding, ongoing, heated, intense, deep disagreement between them. Their argument was continual and it was contentious. They didn't just argue once and then let it go. They argued over and over again. And the more they argued, the angrier they got."
> *Dr. Ray Pritchard,*
> *Keep Believing Ministries*

6. Who did Paul encounter when he arrived at Lystra and what do we learn about him? (Acts 16:1–2)

What else do we learn about this man from the scriptures below?

2 Timothy 1:5

2 Timothy 3:15

7. Paul wanted to bring Timothy along on this missionary journey, but his mixed background of Greek and Jew would have been an issue with the Jews they would encounter along the way. In Acts 16:3 what did Paul decide needed to be done to avoid division or confusion in the mission?

Read 1 Corinthians 9:19–23. How does this help your understanding?

8. How did the decision of the Jerusalem Council enrich ministry with the churches they visited? (Acts 16:4–5)

A DEEPER LOOK

Sharp disagreements between Christians are more common than we'd like to think. And they are always painful. We are called to resolution with our brothers and sisters in Christ, but that can be a difficult process and must be entered into with hearts and minds in the right place.

What does the Bible say about conflict and how to handle it? How do you deal with conflict in your life? What methods lead to successful resolution or even restoration?

Matthew 18:15–17

1 Thessalonians 5:14

2 Timothy 2:23–26

Is there conflict with a fellow believer in your life right now? What is the first step you need to take to resolve the situation? How does Ephesians 4:1–6, 31–32 help?

STUDY FOUR | Acts 16:6–21 | The Call to Macedonia

About 400 miles of travel—on foot—are contained in this section's first five verses for Paul and his companions. The route appears a bit convoluted to human eyes, but the sovereignty of God is the ultimate compass, and Paul was now familiar with the inscrutable ways of his Lord. Paul's vision of a Macedonian man was upended once they reached their destination when the Lord led him instead to a gathering of women on the Sabbath day. The first person chosen by God to open the way for the church beyond the current bounds was a woman about whom rabbis of the day would have said, "It is better that the words of the Law be burned than be delivered to a woman." God was continually shifting paradigms and expectations, as He does still today. He works in and through the least and even the worst of these—and in the lives of Lydia and Paul that kind of extravagant grace was beautifully on display.

---

6 They passed through the Phrygian and Galatian region, having been forbidden by the Holy Spirit to speak the word in Asia; **7** and after they came to Mysia, they were trying to go into Bithynia, and the Spirit of Jesus did not permit them; **8** and passing by Mysia, they came down to Troas. **9** A vision appeared to Paul in the night: a man of Macedonia was standing and appealing to him, and saying, "Come over to Macedonia and help us." **10** When he had seen the vision, immediately we sought to go into Macedonia, concluding that God had called us to preach the gospel to them.

11 So putting out to sea from Troas, we ran a straight course to Samothrace, and on the day following to Neapolis; **12** and from there to Philippi, which is a leading city of the district of Macedonia, a Roman colony; and we were staying in this city for some days. **13** And on the Sabbath day we went outside the gate to a riverside, where we were supposing that there would be a place of prayer; and we sat down and began speaking to the women who had assembled.

14 A woman named Lydia, from the city of Thyatira, a seller of purple fabrics, a worshiper of God, was listening; and the Lord opened her heart to respond to the things spoken by Paul. **15** And when she and her household had been baptized, she urged us, saying, "If you have judged me to be faithful to the Lord, come into my house and stay." And she prevailed upon us.

16 It happened that as we were going to the place of prayer, a slave-girl having a spirit of divination met us, who was bringing her masters much profit by fortune-telling. **17** Following after Paul and us, she kept crying out, saying, "These men are bond-servants of the Most High God, who are proclaiming to you the way of salvation." **18** She continued doing this for many days. But Paul was greatly annoyed, and turned and said to the spirit, "I command you in the name of Jesus Christ to come out of her!" And it came out at that very moment.

19 But when her masters saw that their hope of profit was gone, they seized Paul and Silas and dragged them into the market place before the authorities, **20** and when they had brought them to the chief magistrates, they said, "These men are throwing our city into confusion, being Jews, **21** and are proclaiming customs which it is not lawful for us to accept or to observe, being Romans."

---

1. This is a crucial season in Paul's work, as he progressed on his second missionary journey with Timothy and Silas. Based on verses 6–9, which direction did Paul want to go, and which direction did the Lord want Paul to go?

   How do you see the Holy Spirit at work in these verses?

> The idea of "passing by," in this case, is less a geographical reference and more about where Paul was led to preach. Paul did not stop to teach in every city and town as he was following the Spirit. No explanation is required when we walk in His will; Paul was following the will of God as He purposefully led His servant in proclaiming the Gospel.

2. How does Paul respond in verse 10?

> We see the pronoun change in verse 10 from "he" to "we." This indicates the author, Luke, joined the missionary team, which means much of this record is based on his eyewitness account.

3. How have you experienced the Holy Spirit saying "no" to you? How did you respond? How can a "no" from the Lord sometimes lead to "more than you can ask or think?" (Ephesians 3:20)

4. Where did the team ultimately land in verse 12 and what do we learn about this city?

> Jewish law stated that ten Jewish men who were heads of their household were required to form a synagogue in any city

5. Where does Acts 16:13 tell us Paul and the others went this time and what did they do there?

> In a sermon in 1891, C.H. Spurgeon said this was probably the first religious meeting of Christians that was ever held in Europe.

6. What details are given about the person they encountered in verse 14? What affect did Paul's teaching have that day? (v. 15)

> "During the Roman Period, laws restricted who could wear clothes dyed purple because it was the most precious of all colors. Thus Lydia undoubtedly dealt with an exclusive and affluent clientele." from *The Expository Notes of Dr. Thomas Constable*, which are available online and free.

7. Paul encountered a slave-girl in this city. What do you learn about her and Paul's response to her? (vv. 16–18) Why would Paul respond as he did?

8. How did her owners respond to her healing and what accusations did they make against Paul? (vv. 19–21)

> Magistrates were the chief legal officials of a city responsible for maintaining order. They were also responsible for the temple in Jerusalem and answered to the consuls of Rome. Two were appointed to each colony.

9. How did the slave-girl owners' response to the Gospel differ from Paul's encounter with Lydia?

A DEEPER LOOK

She chose to spend the day in worship and prayer with like-minded friends, so it was evident there was something spiritual already stirring inside Lydia's heart. And yet, she needed one crucial gift to fully believe and respond: "the Lord opened her heart." (v. 14)

The Greek word used here refers to the removal of an obstacle and to give understanding of something that was previously hidden. The concept goes beyond mere explaining or disclosure; it is a supernatural word with supernatural results.

Look up at least ONE of the verses below and write down what happens when God "opens" something that no one else can.

2 Kings 6:17   Luke 24:31–32, 45
Mark 7:33–35   Ephesians 1:18–19

STUDY | Acts 16:22–40
FIVE | A Jailer Becomes Justified

After false accusations and an agitated crowd, Paul and friends find themselves in a familiar place and wait on the Lord with expectant hearts. An act of God set the prisoners free, but Paul decided a chance to proclaim the Gospel to the lost was better than seizing the opportunity to save his own life. After a glorious night, the sun rose on the reality of an uncomfortable situation. The officials wanted to sweep the past day's events under the rug, but Paul wanted their false charges to be examined in the light of truth. A Roman citizen had been wronged, and the hurt inflicted could have ripple effects far beyond this mission team. After one last visit to the fledging Philippian church, Paul departed in peace, leaving behind partners in the Gospel, partakers of grace, and citizens of heaven.

---

22 The crowd rose up together against them, and the chief magistrates tore their robes off them and proceeded to order them to be beaten with rods. **23** When they had struck them with many blows, they threw them into prison, commanding the jailer to guard them securely;**24** and he, having received such a command, threw them into the inner prison and fastened their feet in the stocks.

25 But about midnight Paul and Silas were praying and singing hymns of praise to God, and the prisoners were listening to them; **26** and suddenly there came a great earthquake, so that the foundations of the prison house were shaken; and immediately all the doors were opened and everyone's chains were unfastened. **27** When the jailer awoke and saw the prison doors opened, he drew his sword and was about to kill himself, supposing that the prisoners had escaped. **28** But Paul cried out with a loud voice, saying, "Do not harm yourself, for we are all here!" **29** And he called for lights and rushed in, and trembling with fear he fell down before Paul and Silas, **30** and after he brought them out, he said, "Sirs, what must I do to be saved?"

31 They said, "Believe in the Lord Jesus, and you will be saved, you and your household." **32** And they spoke the word of the Lord to him together with all who were in his house. **33** And he took them that very hour of the night and washed their wounds, and immediately he was baptized, he and all his household. **34** And he brought them into his house and set food before them, and rejoiced greatly, having believed in God with his whole household.

35 Now when day came, the chief magistrates sent their policemen, saying, "Release those men." **36** And the jailer reported these words to Paul, saying, "The chief magistrates have sent to release you. Therefore come out now and go in peace." **37** But Paul said to them, "They have beaten us in public without trial, men who are Romans, and have thrown us into prison; and now are they sending us away secretly? No indeed! But let them come themselves and bring us out." **38** The policemen reported these words to the chief magistrates. They were afraid when they heard that they were Romans, **39** and they came and appealed to them, and when they had brought them out, they kept begging them to leave the city. **40** They went out of the prison and entered the house of Lydia, and when they saw the brethren, they encouraged them and departed.

---

1. What happened to Paul and Silas? (vv. 22–24)

 2. What were Paul and Silas doing while in jail? (see verse 25 and Psalm 42:8)

 3. People were listening to Paul when he was at his best—preaching the Word by the riverside (Acts 16:13–14)—and in the midst of a trial in prison. (v. 25) How does this speak to your life being a witness to those around you? What does this say about the consistency of your walk with Christ?

4. What natural (and supernatural) event occurred in the middle of the night? Who did it affect? How did the jailer respond? How did Paul? (vv. 26–28?)

> When administering a beating with rods, Jewish law mandated forty lashes minus one be given. (2 Corinthians 11:24) The Romans, however, had no limit on the maximum number of blows that could be delivered when beating a person.
>
> ---
>
> In his *New International Commentary on the New Testament*, F.F. Bruce writes that, "These stocks had more than two holes for legs, which could thus be forced apart in a such a way as to cause the utmost discomfort and cramping pain." The inner prison is historically described as a dungeon—without light or fresh air.

Empowered: The Amazing Church of Jesus Christ

5. What choice had Paul made that became evident in verse 28? Choose at least ONE of the verses below and observe how our actions are a tool to proclaim the Gospel.

Matthew 5:16   1 Peter 2:12

1 Corinthians 9:22–23   Titus 2:7–8

Colossians 4:5–6

6. How did Paul's decision impact the jailer? What hope do Paul and Silas give to the jailer? (Acts 16:29–31)

7. Describe the interactions between Paul and Silas and the jailer and his family in verses 32–34.

8. What turn of events takes place in Acts 16:35–36?

9. How did Paul respond and why were the magistrates now afraid of Paul? (vv. 37–38) If Paul had left the city "secretly," what would that have communicated about his character and the young church in Philippi?

> "In the Roman Empire, there were two very different laws: one for citizens of the Roman Empire, and one for those who were not citizens. Roman citizens had specific civil rights which were zealously guarded. Non-citizens had no civil rights, and were subject to the whims of both the multitude and the magistrates." from the *NET Bible*

10. What did Paul do in verse 40 before complying with the magistrates' request? Why was that an important visit?

A DEEPER LOOK

There are two gestures of hospitality offered as a result of salvation in this passage. What are they? (Acts 16:15, 33–34)

In her book *The Gospel Comes With A House Key*, Rosaria Butterfield defines hospitality for Christians as both "radical and ordinary"—a practice that uses "your Christian home in a daily way that seeks to make strangers neighbors, and neighbors family of God. It brings glory to God, serves others, and lives out the gospel in word and deed."

What does God's Word say about the importance of practicing hospitality?

Luke 14:12–14
Romans 16:1–2   Hebrews 13:16
Galatians 6:10   1 Peter 4:8–11

When was the last time you offered hospitality in a manner reflective of the gospel? What happened?

Week 8 Teaching Notes

Map of Paul's Second Missionary Journey

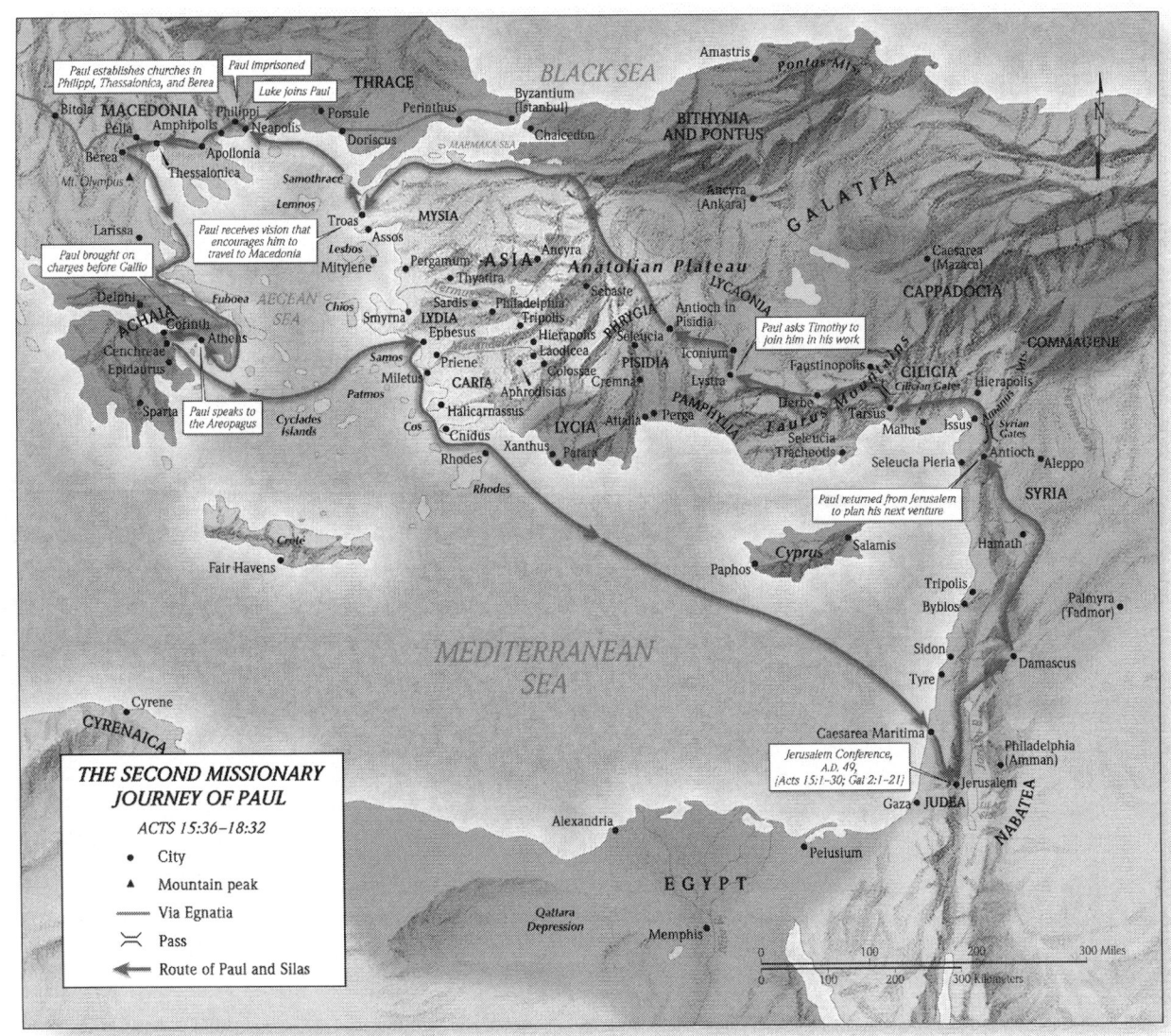

THE SECOND MISSIONARY
JOURNEY OF PAUL

ACTS 15:36–18:32

- • City
- ▲ Mountain peak
- Via Egnatia
- ⋈ Pass
- ← Route of Paul and Silas

Empowered: The Amazing Church of Jesus Christ

Acts 17:1–18:22

Christianity Spreads from Macedonia to Achaia

By this time in his life, Paul's ministry was a living picture of what it means to "run the race." He always waited on God to work by His Spirit, but he also knew what had to be done to reach the lost, and he did it—over and over and over. Rather than pitch his tent and wait for someone to wander in, Paul went looking for those who needed to hear of the hope and grace offered by his Savior. He travelled thousands of miles on his second missionary journey with one intention in his heart: to spread the good news of Jesus. And his message was embraced and rejected in equal measure.

Paul proclaimed Christ without hesitation or error in the civic, religious, and public venues of the day. While passionate, Paul remained rational; every point had a purpose and every answer was grounded in truth. He was steadfast, but still human. We see him discouraged and fearful in the face of fierce opposition. And we are encouraged knowing even "the great Paul" sometimes wanted to give up and go home.

Paul's faithful, reasoned presentation of the Gospel is a good example for us as we live under the call of Acts 1:8 every day. But the greater blessing is watching our faithful God hold fast to those who labor in the name of Love. This week, we see many obtain the imperishable prize of salvation, but we also walk with Paul through difficult days. We rejoice in victories won by grace and are spurred on by the hope of fruit from perseverance and comfort in fear that God promised to His servant—because they are for us, too.

KEY VERSE:

"And according to Paul's custom, he went to them, and for three Sabbaths reasoned with them from the Scriptures, explaining and giving evidence that the Christ had to suffer and rise again from the dead, and saying, 'This Jesus whom I am proclaiming to you is the Christ.'"

ACTS 17:2–3

STUDY ONE | Acts 17:1–9 | The Gospel in Thessalonica

We travel 100 miles with Paul in verse 1 and watch him continue his pattern of preaching to the Jews first. There is helpful commentary in this passage describing how Paul chose to proclaim this message. It is instructive to see that you can be passionate about something without overwhelming (some might say, "Bible beating") those you hope to win over. After all, we know that faith is a gift. (Ephesians 2:8–9) And rather than a compelling story or lofty explanations convincing people into the Kingdom, 1 Corinthians 2:4 tells us sharing the Gospel is all about God's power and Spirit at work, drawing those with open hearts to Himself.

---

1 Now when they had traveled through Amphipolis and Apollonia, they came to Thessalonica, where there was a synagogue of the Jews. **2** And according to Paul's custom, he went to them, and for three Sabbaths reasoned with them from the Scriptures, **3** explaining and giving evidence that the Christ had to suffer and rise again from the dead, and saying, "This Jesus whom I am proclaiming to you is the Christ." **4** And some of them were persuaded and joined Paul and Silas, along with a large number of the God-fearing Greeks and a number of the leading women. **5** But the Jews, becoming jealous and taking along some wicked men from the market place, formed a mob and set the city in an uproar; and attacking the house of Jason, they were seeking to bring them out to the people. **6** When they did not find them, they began dragging Jason and some brethren before the city authorities, shouting, "These men who have upset the world have come here also; **7** and Jason has welcomed them, and they all act contrary to the decrees of Caesar, saying that there is another king, Jesus." **8** They stirred up the crowd and the city authorities who heard these things. **9** And when they had received a pledge from Jason and the others, they released them.

---

1. Where did Paul and Silas go when they arrived in Thessalonica? (vv. 1–2)

 2. Circle the timeframe and action words used to describe Paul's method of evangelism in verses 2–3.

> Thessalonica was the most heavily populated city of the area. It was a major seaport, important commercial center, and the location of several important trade routes. Thessalonica was predominately Greek but controlled by Rome. It was the capital of the province of Macedonia.

3. What was the "thesis" of Paul's argument in verse 3?

Empowered: The Amazing Church of Jesus Christ

4. Why is Paul's three-step approach of "reasoning, explaining, and giving evidence" in sharing the Gospel so effective?

5. As we've seen throughout Paul's ministry so far, there were generally two responses to his message. What do we see in verses 4–5?

6. What motivated the Jews to slander Paul, and how did the situation escalate in verse 5? (Read 1 Corinthians 1:18–25 as a commentary on this scene.)

7. How did they describe Paul's ministry in Acts 17:6? Could this be said about Christians or the Church today? Why or why not? (see also the ESV translation of this verse)

8. What was the crowd's accusation in verse 7? How does this compare to Luke 23:1–2? Who were the charges against at that time?

9. What happened to Jason as a result of his association with Paul? (Acts 17:6–9)

> "Pledge" in verse 9 refers to a bond posted by Jason that would be forfeited if Paul and Silas did not immediately leave the city.

A DEEPER LOOK

Reason, explanation, and proofs are solid strategies for presenting the Gospel to unbelievers. But that's not all that's required to comprehend Scripture. Choose at least ONE of the verses below and determine what else the Bible tells us we need to be able to examine and understand His Word.

Psalm 119:18

John 14:26

1 Corinthians 2:6–16

2 Timothy 2:7

STUDY TWO | Acts 17:10–21
The Gospel in Berea and Athens

In today's passage, Paul engaged in two unique opportunities that took place more than 200 miles apart: Jews eager to study the Scriptures with open hearts and minds, and Greeks who were open to Paul's "new" idea about a man being raised from the dead. This was Paul's most receptive Jewish audience yet, but the access was short-lived, cut off by outsiders with an ax to grind. So he fled to the home of Socrates, Plato, and Aristotle, and found himself surrounded by unparalleled beauty and knowledge. But the deep-rooted idolatry that permeated the city was all that Paul could see. He conversed with the great minds of the day and welcomed the opportunity to expand their understanding of what true worship was all about.

---

10 The brethren immediately sent Paul and Silas away by night to Berea, and when they arrived, they went into the synagogue of the Jews. **11** Now these were more noble-minded than those in Thessalonica, for they received the word with great eagerness, examining the Scriptures daily to see whether these things were so. **12** Therefore many of them believed, along with a number of prominent Greek women and men. **13** But when the Jews of Thessalonica found out that the word of God had been proclaimed by Paul in Berea also, they came there as well, agitating and stirring up the crowds. **14** Then immediately the brethren sent Paul out to go as far as the sea; and Silas and Timothy remained there. **15** Now those who escorted Paul brought him as far as Athens; and receiving a command for Silas and Timothy to come to him as soon as possible, they left. **16** Now while Paul was waiting for them at Athens, his spirit was being provoked within him as he was observing the city full of idols. **17** So he was reasoning in the synagogue with the Jews and the God-fearing Gentiles, and in the market place every day with those who happened to be present. **18** And also some of the Epicurean and Stoic philosophers were conversing with him. Some were saying, "What would this idle babbler wish to say?" Others, "He seems to be a proclaimer of strange deities,"—because he was preaching Jesus and the resurrection. **19** And they took him and brought him to the Areopagus, saying, "May we know what this new teaching is which you are proclaiming? **20** For you are bringing some strange things to our ears; so we want to know what these things mean." **21** (Now all the Athenians and the strangers visiting there used to spend their time in nothing other than telling or hearing something new.)

---

1. Where did Paul go next and why? What evidence do you see that they were not deterred in their mission? (v. 10)

2. What do you see that would have been encouraging to Paul and Silas in verses 11–12?

3. There always seems to be an opposition to the message of the Gospel. This time it came from an interesting source. Who was it? (v. 13)

4. Where did Paul go next and who went with him? (vv. 14–15)

5. What does verse 16 tell us was particularly disturbing to Paul in this place? What did he do about it? (v. 17)

6. An additional context is mentioned for Paul's missionary efforts in verse 17. Where did he go and who might he have encountered there that he might not have at a synagogue?

7. Look up Epicurean and Stoic philosophies. Write down what you learn about each below.

▶ Epicureans

▶ Stoics

8. What are the challenges inherent in proclaiming the gospel to people who think differently from you?

 9. List the responses of the hearers in verses 18–20.

What was their motivation in wanting to learn more? (Acts 17:21)

A DEEPER LOOK

Name some common objections you could receive when sharing the Gospel with someone.

What could be your response to each one of those objections? Consider what Scripture you might use to support your objections.

STUDY THREE | Acts 17:22–34
Paul's Sermon at Mars Hill

Paul was a zealous evangelist, but he was also compassionate and wise. And nowhere is this better demonstrated than in his discourse in the Areopagus. Here, rather than choosing to denounce and condemn, Paul met lost souls right where they were and labored to lead them home. He didn't preach of a God who hated them for their idolatry, nor did he sentence them to hell for their rebellion and pride. Instead, he painted a picture of a God who is as close as their brother or friend, a King who wants to reign in their hearts rather than on a throne; a God who gives rather than demands, creates out of pleasure, cares about the details of lives, and calls us His children. This God cannot be formed or conjured up, he told them, and once you belong to Him, nothing on earth will satisfy.

---

22 So Paul stood in the midst of the Areopagus and said, "Men of Athens, I observe that you are very religious in all respects. **23** For while I was passing

Empowered: The Amazing Church of Jesus Christ

through and examining the objects of your worship, I also found an altar with this inscription, 'TO AN UNKNOWN GOD.' Therefore what you worship in ignorance, this I proclaim to you. **24** The God who made the world and all things in it, since He is Lord of heaven and earth, does not dwell in temples made with hands; **25** nor is He served by human hands, as though He needed anything, since He Himself gives to all people life and breath and all things; **26** and He made from one man every nation of mankind to live on all the face of the earth, having determined their appointed times and the boundaries of their habitation, **27** that they would seek God, if perhaps they might grope for Him and find Him, though He is not far from each one of us; **28** for in Him we live and move and exist, as even some of your own poets have said, 'For we also are His children.' **29** Being then the children of God, we ought not to think that the Divine Nature is like gold or silver or stone, an image formed by the art and thought of man. **30** Therefore having overlooked the times of ignorance, God is now declaring to men that all people everywhere should repent, **31** because He has fixed a day in which He will judge the world in righteousness through a Man whom He has appointed, having furnished proof to all men by raising Him from the dead." **32** Now when they heard of the resurrection of the dead, some began to sneer, but others said, "We shall hear you again concerning this." **33** So Paul went out of their midst. **34** But some men joined him and believed, among whom also were Dionysius the Areopagite and a woman named Damaris and others with them.

---

1. How did Paul describe the "men of Athens" in verse 22? How was this portrayal strategic when viewed in light of verse 16?

2. What does verse 23 indicate Paul was doing? How would this be helpful to him in his ministry to these people?

3. In verses 24–28, Paul introduces his attentive audience to their "unknown god."

   What attributes of God do you see in verses 24–25?

> Mars Hill is Latin for *Areopagus.* The name is based on a myth that Mars or Ares, in Greek—the Roman god of war, was tried here by the gods for killing Poseidon's son. In Paul's day, Mars Hill served as the meeting place for the Areopagus Court, the highest court in Greece for civil, criminal, and religious matters. Even under Roman rule in the time of the New Testament, Mars Hill remained an important meeting place where philosophy, religion, and law were discussed. (from gotquestions.org)

How is God's relationship with man described in verses 26–28?

4. Read Psalm 115:4–8. Contrast that description of idols with what Paul says about God in Acts 17:24–28.

5. What warnings and admonitions does Paul give in Acts 17:29–31?

6. Paul references one man in verse 26 and one man in verse 31. Who are these two men and what do they represent?

7. Acts 17:32–34 contain three responses to the Gospel message. What are they? Give examples of these kinds of responses that you have faced in your life and experience.

8. Paul is a great example for us in the way he shared his faith as he followed God's specific call on his life. As believers, we all fall under the call and commission of Acts 1:8. What can you learn from Paul and his ministry? How do you talk about your faith with others?

9. What are the "gods" of our culture today?

A DEEPER LOOK

Paul spends his time at Mars Hill specifically defining the "unknown god" the Athenians worshipped. One of the many ways our Creator God is different from man-made gods is that He is alive and wants to have a relationship with His creation.

Choose at least ONE verse and answer: what does Scripture tell us about how God makes Himself *known* to us?

Exodus 34:5–7   John 1:14
Deuteronomy 4:29–31   Romans 1:19–20
Psalm 19:1–2   1 John 4:7–9

How has God specifically made Himself known to you?

STUDY FOUR | Acts 18:1–11
Paul in Corinth with Priscilla and Aquila

Kindred spirits. Cut from the same cloth. That must have been how Paul felt when he met Priscilla and Aquila. They knew what it was like to be forced from familiarity and rejected by those around you. This couple was 600 miles from everything they knew, and Paul became instant family. But a tense encounter with an ungodly and irreverent group discouraged Paul so much he was tempted to pack it all in. It is unusual to see this trailblazing evangelist shrink back in the face of fear. God's words of assurance refreshed Paul's spirit, and he settled in to seek out and find the ones God was calling into His kingdom.

---

1 After these things he left Athens and went to Corinth. **2** And he found a Jew named Aquila, a native of Pontus, having recently come from Italy with his wife Priscilla, because Claudius had commanded all the Jews to leave Rome. He came to them, **3** and because he was of the same trade, he stayed with them and they were working, for by trade they were tent-makers. **4** And he was reasoning in the synagogue every Sabbath and trying to persuade Jews and Greeks.

5 But when Silas and Timothy came down from Macedonia, Paul began devoting himself completely to the word, solemnly testifying to the Jews that Jesus was the Christ. **6** But when they resisted and blasphemed, he shook out his garments and said to them, "Your blood be on your own heads! I am clean. From now on I will go to the Gentiles." **7** Then he left there and went to the house of a man named Titius Justus, a worshiper of God, whose house was next to the synagogue. **8** Crispus, the leader of the synagogue, believed in the Lord with all his household, and many of the Corinthians when they heard were believing and being baptized. **9** And the Lord said to Paul in the night by a vision, "Do not be afraid any longer, but go on speaking and do not be silent; **10** for I am with you, and no man will attack you in order to harm you, for I have many people in this city." **11** And he settled there a year and six months, teaching the word of God among them.

1. Next, Paul travels forty-six miles west to Corinth. Who does he encounter there and why are they there? (v. 2)

> At this time, Corinth was the fourth largest city in the world, fifty miles west of and about twenty times larger than Athens. It was located on the southern tip of Greece between two ports, giving it great commercial and military importance. The Temple of Aphrodite was located here along with 1,000 temple prostitutes.

2. What do Priscilla and Aquila have in common with Paul? (vv. 2–3) What else do we learn about them in Romans 16:3–5?

3. When Paul wasn't earning a living, what did he continue to do? (Acts 18:4)

4. Who arrives on the scene in verse 5? According to 2 Corinthians 11:9, what did they bring? What was the impact? (Acts 18:5)

5. Who was Paul specifically trying to reach in Corinth? How did they respond to him in Acts 18:5–6?

6. Read Ezekiel 3:16–19 below. How does this speak to Paul's situation in Acts 18:6–7?

> "At the end of seven days the word of the Lord came to me saying, 'Son of man, I have appointed you a watchman to the house of Israel; whenever you hear a word from my mouth, warn them from Me. When I say to the wicked, "You will surely die," and you do not warn him or speak out to warn the wicked from his wicked way that he may live, that wicked man shall die in his iniquity, but his blood I will require at your hand. Yet if you have warned the wicked and he does not turn from his wickedness or from his wicked way, he shall die in his iniquity; you have delivered yourself.'"

7. What happened as a result of Paul's move? (Acts 18:8)

8. How did the Lord encourage His servant in verses 9–10?

9. What do we learn Paul did in verse 11?

A DEEPER LOOK

There are many other examples in Scripture of the Lord encouraging His servants.
Fill in the chart below and then answer the questions that follow.

Who needed encouragement?	Shared exhortation	What did God promise?
Genesis 15:1 _____		
Genesis 26:17, 24 _____		
Genesis 46:2–4 _____		
2 Chronicles 20:15–17 _____		
Daniel 10:12,19 _____		
Luke 1:30 _____		

What do God's promises and assurances tell you about the heart of mankind across the ages?

What does this teach you about God?

How do these reminders from Scripture encourage you today?

STUDY FIVE | Acts 18:12–22 | Gallio's Uprising

When a united group of Jews brought a familiar complaint against Paul to Gallio, the Roman governor of the province, the leader remained impartial. No law has been broken, he told them, and he refused to involve himself in an issue that had nothing to do with Rome. Scholars say this decision set a precedent for the other proconsuls of the region that provided protection for Christianity and allowed it to spread throughout the Roman Empire until Nero rose to power. The Jews took out their anger instead on an innocent man, the second synagogue leader drawn to Christ through Paul's ministry (18:8). As his second missionary journey comes to a close, Paul heads eastward and ends where he began.

---

12 But while Gallio was proconsul of Achaia, the Jews with one accord rose up against Paul and brought him before the judgment seat, **13** saying, "This man persuades men to worship God contrary to the law." **14** But when Paul was about to open his mouth, Gallio said to the Jews, "If it were a matter of wrong or of vicious crime, O Jews, it would be reasonable for me to put up with you; **15** but if there are questions about words and names and your own law, look after it yourselves; I am unwilling to be a judge of these matters." **16** And he drove them away from the judgment seat. **17** And they all took hold of Sosthenes, the leader of the synagogue, and began beating him in front of the judgment seat. But Gallio was not concerned about any of these things.

18 Paul, having remained many days longer, took leave of the brethren and put out to sea for Syria, and with him were Priscilla and Aquila. In Cenchrea he had his hair cut, for he was keeping a vow. **19** They came to Ephesus, and he left them there. Now he himself entered the synagogue and reasoned with the Jews. **20** When they asked him to stay for a longer time, he did not consent, **21** but taking leave of them and saying, "I will return to you again if God wills," he set sail from Ephesus.

22 When he had landed at Caesarea, he went up and greeted the church, and went down to Antioch.

Empowered: The Amazing Church of Jesus Christ

1. How was Paul's ministry interrupted in verses 12–13?

2. What unusual turn of events do you see in verses 14–16?

> Gallio was proconsul of Achaia in 51–52 A.D., information that helps date not only Paul's time in Corinth but the time frame of his second missionary journey as well. Interestingly, Gallio's brother was the famed Stoic philosopher, Seneca, who was Nero's tutor.

3. How did God use Gallio to fulfill His promises from verse 10?

4. Where did Paul go next and with whom? (v. 18) What was their ultimate destination? (v. 19)

5. What cities has Paul set his sights on in Acts 18:19–22?

> From an act of gratitude to seeking God's blessing on a ministry endeavor, scholars differ on what Paul's vow might have been about. The greater point is, Paul did not forsake his Jewishness while fully embracing new life in Christ. This also could have served as an example for other Jews who were struggling with the Law and grace. For more information about the purpose of Nazarite vows, see Numbers 6:1–12.

6. Paul endured several difficult encounters in our study this week (17:5, 13, 18; 18: 6, 12–13). What do the verses below (the words of Jesus Himself!) say that would be a help and encouragement to Paul, or anyone in a similar situation?

   Matthew 5:10–12

7. Paul was angered and discouraged by the response of the Jews in Corinth, but as his second missionary journey comes to an end, we see he persists in trying to reach his own people with the hope of Christ.

   Choose at least ONE of the verses on the next page to read as a reminder of how strongly Paul felt about the message he was spreading and the lengths he was willing to go to see hearts and lives changed for eternity.

Romans 1:13–16
Romans 9:2–5
1 Corinthians 9:16, 19–23

2 Corinthians 12:15a
Philippians 1:12–14
2 Timothy 2:8–10

 8. What do you learn about Paul's heart for his people? How does this reflect the heart of God?

9. This marks the end of Paul's second missionary journey. Paul travelled approximately 2,800 miles, on water and land, over three years. Review the map at the beginning of this chapter (page 130) and use a colored pen or pencil to trace Paul's journey.

10. Church planting is one way to grow numbers in the Church. How does personal evangelism grow the Church?

Empowered: The Amazing Church of Jesus Christ

WEEK 9 TEACHING NOTES

Map of Paul's Third Missionary Journey

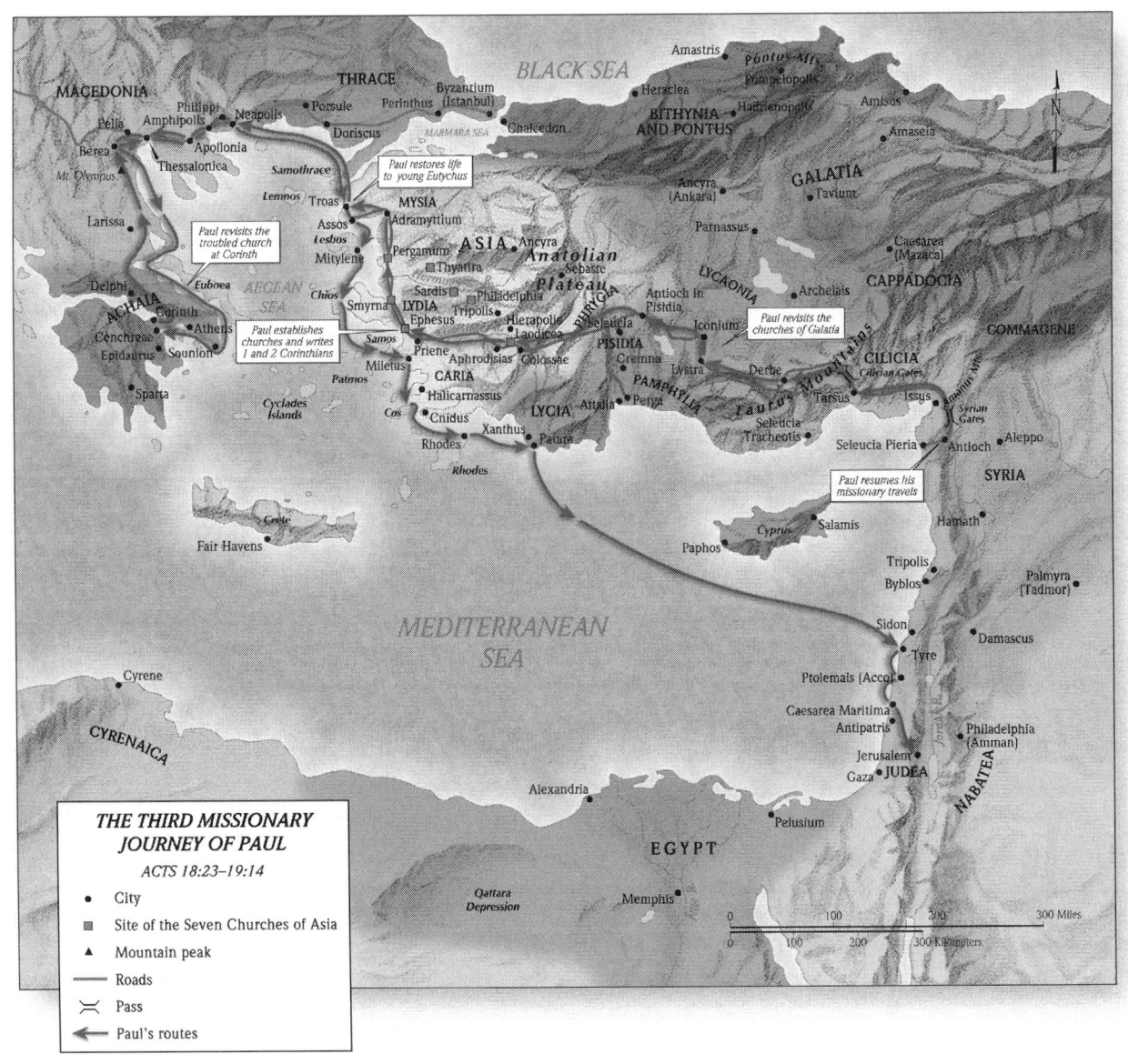

THE THIRD MISSIONARY JOURNEY OF PAUL
ACTS 18:23–19:14

- • City
- ▣ Site of the Seven Churches of Asia
- ▲ Mountain peak
- ⌇ Roads
- ⋈ Pass
- ⟵ Paul's routes

Empowered: The Amazing Church of Jesus Christ

Acts 18:23–21:16

Paul's Third Missionary Journey

There are some things about Paul's third missionary journey that are measured and quantified in Scripture: from 52–57 A.D., Paul traveled approximately 2,700 miles, stopped in seventeen cities, and spent three years ministering in one place. He exorcised demons, defied idolatry, and raised the dead. He preached the Gospel and made disciples in the synagogues and city streets, in lecture halls and on the seashore.

And while God's Word is complete, the coverage of Paul's journey is not comprehensive. There are some things that only heaven knows—like how many hours Paul spent in prayer, how he battled through discouragement and exhaustion. And how many lives were changed forever because of his genuine love for others and faithful obedience to his Savior.

But Paul never measured the value of his own life along the way. He determined that every mile travelled, miracle performed, and truth proclaimed would point to the infinite worth of Christ and the life-saving power of the Gospel.

Paul was always single-minded—"to testify solemnly of the gospel of the grace of God"—but, in these passages, his focus narrows even more. The Holy Spirit was leading Paul to Jerusalem and Rome, and he was prepared to finish his course.

KEY VERSE:

"But I do not consider my life of any account as dear to myself, so that I may finish my course and the ministry which I received from the Lord Jesus, to testify solemnly of the gospel of the grace of God."

ACTS 20:24

STUDY ONE | Acts 18:23–19:20
Helping Those Who Believed

When it comes to truth, almost right is often the same as completely wrong. We see examples of this in our passage, as Paul and a faithful ministry couple encountered disciples who had good intentions but incomplete understanding. Gentle re-teaching corrected their paths and opened the door for the Gospel to spread. Paul's bold teaching in Ephesus attracted friends, enemies, and counterfeit Christians who misused the name of Jesus to benefit themselves. When the story about a demon casting out exorcists circulated among the Ephesians, revival took place. Hearts were turned and many watched their formerly wicked way of life go up in flames as the word of the Lord continued to overcome the darkness.

---

23 And having spent some time there, he left and passed successively through the Galatian region and Phrygia, strengthening all the disciples.

24 Now a Jew named Apollos, an Alexandrian by birth, an eloquent man, came to Ephesus; and he was mighty in the Scriptures. 25 This man had been instructed in the way of the Lord; and being fervent in spirit, he was speaking and teaching accurately the things concerning Jesus, being acquainted only with the baptism of John; 26 and he began to speak out boldly in the synagogue. But when Priscilla and Aquila heard him, they took him aside and explained to him the way of God more accurately. 27 And when he wanted to go across to Achaia, the brethren encouraged him and wrote to the disciples to welcome him; and when he had arrived, he greatly helped those who had believed through grace, 28 for he powerfully refuted the Jews in public, demonstrating by the Scriptures that Jesus was the Christ.

19 1 It happened that while Apollos was at Corinth, Paul passed through the upper country and came to Ephesus, and found some disciples. 2 He said to them, "Did you receive the Holy Spirit when you believed?" And they said to him, "No, we have not even heard whether there is a Holy Spirit." 3 And he said, "Into what then were you baptized?" And they said, "Into John's baptism." 4 Paul said, "John baptized with the baptism of repentance, telling the people to believe in Him who was coming after him, that is, in Jesus." 5 When they heard this, they were baptized in the name of the Lord Jesus. 6 And when Paul had laid his hands upon them, the Holy Spirit came on them, and they began speaking with tongues and prophesying. 7 There were in all about twelve men.

8 And he entered the synagogue and continued speaking out boldly for three months, reasoning and persuading them about the kingdom of God. 9 But when some were becoming hardened and disobedient, speaking evil of the Way before the people, he withdrew from them and took away the disciples, reasoning daily in the school of Tyrannus. 10 This took place for two years, so that all who lived in Asia heard the word of the Lord, both Jews and Greeks.

11 God was performing extraordinary miracles by the hands of Paul, 12 so that handkerchiefs or aprons were even carried from his body to the sick, and the diseases left them and the evil spirits went out. 13 But also some of the Jewish exorcists, who went from place to place, attempted to name over those who had the evil spirits the name of the Lord Jesus, saying, "I adjure you by Jesus whom Paul preaches." 14 Seven sons of one Sceva, a Jewish chief priest, were doing this. 15 And the evil spirit answered and said to them, "I recognize Jesus, and I know about Paul, but who are you?" 16 And the man, in whom was the evil spirit, leaped on them and subdued all of them and overpowered them, so that they fled out of that house naked and wounded. 17 This became known to all, both Jews and Greeks, who lived in Ephesus; and fear fell upon

Empowered: The Amazing Church of Jesus Christ

them all and the name of the Lord Jesus was being magnified. **18** Many also of those who had believed kept coming, confessing and disclosing their practices. **19** And many of those who practiced magic brought their books together and began burning them in the sight of everyone; and they counted up the price of them and found it fifty thousand pieces of silver. **20** So the word of the Lord was growing mightily and prevailing.

---

1. Verse 24 could begin, "Meanwhile, back in Ephesus…" as it points us back to Acts 18:19, when Paul visited Ephesus for the first time and left his friends Priscilla and Aquila to establish ministry. Who do we meet in verse 24 and what do we learn about his gifts?

> Alexandria in Egypt was the center of culture and academia at the time. The city was home to a university and a library that contained more than 500,000 volumes. Jewish rabbis produced the Septuagint, the Greek translation of the Old Testament, there in 132 B.C.

2. How would 2 Timothy 4:2 have been instructive and emboldening for people like Priscilla and Aquila?

3. How is 2 Timothy 2:15 instructive for someone like Apollos?

4. What can we infer from the following verses about the overall ministry of Apollos and how it impacted the growth of the Church?

"For when one says, 'I am of Paul,' and another, 'I am of Apollos,' are you not mere men? What then is Apollos? And what is Paul? Servants through whom you believed, even as the Lord gave opportunity to each one. I planted, Apollos watered, but God was causing the growth. So then neither the one who plants nor the one who waters is anything, but God who causes the growth."
1 Corinthians 3:4–7

"But concerning Apollos our brother, I encouraged him greatly to come to you with the brethren; and it was not at all his desire to come now, but he will come when he has opportunity."
1 Corinthians 16:12

"Diligently help Zenas the lawyer and Apollos on their way so that nothing is lacking for them."
Titus 3:13

5. We rejoin Paul on his third journey in Acts 19:1, as he returns to Ephesus. In Acts 19:1–2, Paul has an experience similar to Priscilla and Aquila. What is notable about the disciples he finds in verses 1–2?

6. How does he help "complete" their faith? (vv. 4–5) What evidence is given to confirm their salvation? (v. 6)

> This is the last mention of speaking in tongues in the book of Acts.

7. Paul continues his pattern of ministry in verse 8. What three words or phrases are used to describe those who opposed Paul and the Gospel in verse 9?

8. What was God doing through Paul in Ephesus? (vv. 11–12)

 9. One event had a significant impact on the lives of "all, both Jews and Greeks" in Ephesus. What was it and what was their initial response? (vv. 13–17)

> In his commentary on Acts, Dr. Darrell Bock estimates that 50,000 drachmas represents nearly $6 million in today's currency.

 10. The Holy Spirit continued to actively work in the hearts of the Ephesian believers. How did those practicing magic respond to His conviction of sin? (v. 19)

A DEEPER LOOK

We saw two examples in this passage of incomplete faith resulting from incomplete or inaccurate instruction. Why is the teaching of sound doctrine important, according to the verses below? Choose AT LEAST one to help guide your thinking.

1 Timothy 4:6–13   2 Timothy 2:14–16, 23–26
1 Timothy 6:20   2 Timothy 3:14–17
2 Timothy 1:13–14   2 Timothy 4:1–5

Demetrius had a bone to pick with Paul. For years, Demetrius had done well for himself, crafting and selling graven images to pilgrims who came to worship the great Artemis. But Paul's proclamation of truth and life challenged everything he thought he knew. Chaos and confusion are hallmarks of the enemy, and his evil schemes were on full display in a rioting mob's blind rage. The crowd would've killed Paul if not for a sovereign intervention. Personal gain was the catalyst of this mayhem, but pockets full of cash pale in comparison to the blessings freely given by the one true God.

---

21 Now after these things were finished, Paul purposed in the Spirit to go to Jerusalem after he had passed through Macedonia and Achaia, saying, "After I have been there, I must also see Rome." 22 And having sent into Macedonia two of those who ministered to him, Timothy and Erastus, he himself stayed in Asia for a while.

23 About that time there occurred no small disturbance concerning the Way. 24 For a man named Demetrius, a silversmith, who made silver shrines of Artemis, was bringing no little business to the craftsmen; 25 these he gathered together with the workmen of similar trades, and said, "Men, you know that our prosperity depends upon this business. 26 You see and hear that not only in Ephesus, but in almost all of Asia, this Paul has persuaded and turned away a considerable number of people, saying that gods made with hands are no gods at all. 27 Not only is there danger that this trade of ours fall into disrepute, but also that the temple of the great goddess Artemis be regarded as worthless and that she whom all of Asia and the world worship will even be dethroned from her magnificence."

28 When they heard this and were filled with rage, they began crying out, saying, "Great is Artemis of the Ephesians!" 29 The city was filled with the confusion, and they rushed with one accord into the theater, dragging along Gaius and Aristarchus, Paul's traveling companions from Macedonia. 30 And when Paul wanted to go into the assembly, the disciples would not let him. 31 Also some of the Asiarchs who were friends of his sent to him and repeatedly urged him not to venture into the theater. 32 So then, some were shouting one thing and some another, for the assembly was in confusion and the majority did not know for what reason they had come together. 33 Some of the crowd concluded it was Alexander, since the Jews had put him forward; and having motioned with his hand, Alexander was intending to make a defense to the assembly. 34 But when they recognized that he was a Jew, a single outcry arose from them all as they shouted for about two hours, "Great is Artemis of the Ephesians!" 35 After quieting the crowd, the town clerk said, "Men of Ephesus, what man is there after all who does not know that the city of the Ephesians is guardian of the temple of the great Artemis and of the image which fell down from heaven? 36 So, since these are undeniable facts, you ought to keep calm and to do nothing rash. 37 For you have brought these men here who are neither robbers of temples nor blasphemers of our goddess.

38 So then, if Demetrius and the craftsmen who are with him have a complaint against any man, the courts are in session and proconsuls are available; let them bring charges against one another. **39** But if you want anything beyond this, it shall be settled in the lawful assembly. **40** For indeed we are in danger of being accused of a riot in connection with today's events, since there is no real cause for it, and in this connection we will be unable to account for this disorderly gathering." **41** After saying this he dismissed the assembly.

---

1. Paul had two major, ultimate destinations in mind in verse 21. What were they?

   Jesus' resolve about carrying out His purpose on earth was recorded in Luke 9:51—"When the days were approaching for His ascension, He was determined to go to Jerusalem." The Greek word for "determined" literally means, "set His face." How does this verse help you interpret Paul's intent in Acts 19:21?

> Paul wrote his first letter to the Corinthian church during this time and sent the letter with Timothy and Erastus in verse 22.

2. Who was Demetrius? What were his concerns about Christianity, or "the Way?" (vv. 23–27)

> Historians record that the Temple of Artemis—or Diana—was one of the seven wonders of the ancient world and was the center for worship of this Roman fertility goddess. The temple was 100 feet by 340 feet and contained 177 columns that were fifty-five feet tall and six feet thick. It could hold between 25,000–50,000 people. There were thirty-three shrines to Artemis across the Roman Empire, but Ephesus was the center of worship. By 401 A.D., the temple had been completely destroyed.

3. What does his speech to his fellow craftsmen tell you about the economy of Ephesus?

4. Read Isaiah 44:9–11 below:

   "Those who fashion a graven image are all of them futile, and their precious things are of no profit; even their own witnesses fail to see or know, so that they will be put to shame. Who has fashioned a god or cast an idol to no profit? Behold, all his companions will be put to shame, for the craftsmen themselves are mere men. Let them all assemble themselves, let them stand up, let them tremble, let them together be put to shame."

   What was this idol-maker's idol?

5. Paul is known for presenting the case for Christ in a measured, reasoned, rational fashion. How do the Ephesians present their opposing view and how does the crowd respond? (vv. 32–34)

6. What does 1 Corinthians 14:33a tell us about the origin of chaos and confusion—"For God is not a God of confusion but of peace...?"

7. In Acts 19:35, the town clerk—similar to today's mayor—quieted the mob. According to the clerk, of what crime was Paul guilty? (vv. 35–37)

8. What was the illegal activity taking place according to the laws of Rome? (v. 40)

STUDY THREE | Acts 20:1–16
A Sleepy Saint

This section of Scripture is best known for the sleepy saint who met his untimely end, then experienced the grace of God by the hand of Paul. As pastor-teacher, Paul only served solid food to the brethren, and even if it was a lot to take in, he knew it was the only way to sustain the Church. Paul penned several letters—1 and 2 Corinthians and Romans—during the time period in this passage, never wasting a moment when souls were at stake. Persecution continued to follow Paul, but never distracted him. His mind was on his mission. And the number of names and places in these sixteen verses indicates he kept his commitment to cover much ground and bring people to their Savior at every opportunity.

---

20 After the uproar had ceased, Paul sent for the disciples, and when he had exhorted them and taken his leave of them, he left to go to Macedonia. **2** When he had gone through those districts and had given them much exhortation, he came to Greece. **3** And there he spent three months, and when a plot was formed against him by the Jews as he was about to set sail for Syria, he decided to return through Macedonia. **4** And he was accompanied by Sopater of Berea, the son of Pyrrhus, and by Aristarchus and Secundus of the Thessalonians, and Gaius of Derbe, and Timothy, and Tychicus and Trophimus of Asia. **5** But these had gone on ahead and were waiting for us at Troas. **6** We sailed from Philippi after the days of Unleavened Bread, and came to them at Troas within five days; and there we stayed seven days.

7 On the first day of the week, when we were gathered together to break bread, Paul began talking to them, intending to leave the next day, and he prolonged his message until midnight. **8** There were many lamps in the upper room where we were gathered together. **9** And there was a young man named Eutychus sitting on the window sill, sinking into a deep sleep; and as Paul kept on talking, he was overcome by sleep and fell down from the third floor and was picked up dead. **10** But Paul went down and fell upon him, and after embracing him, he said, "Do not be troubled, for his life is in him." **11** When he had gone back up and had broken the bread and eaten, he talked with them a long while until daybreak, and then left. **12** They took away the boy alive, and were greatly comforted.

13 But we, going ahead to the ship, set sail for Assos, intending from there to take Paul on board; for so he had arranged it, intending himself to go by land. **14** And when he met us at Assos, we took him on board and came to Mitylene. **15** Sailing from there, we arrived the following day opposite Chios; and the next day we crossed over to Samos; and the day following we came to Miletus. **16** For Paul had decided to sail past Ephesus so that he would not have to spend time in Asia; for he was hurrying to be in Jerusalem, if possible, on the day of Pentecost.

---

1. What was the first thing Paul did after the Ephesians' rioting calmed down? (v. 1)

2. Read Paul's words to Timothy in the verse below. How does it enlighten us about Paul's ministry strategy with the men in Acts 20:4?

   "The things which you have heard from me in the presence of many witnesses, entrust these to faithful men who will be able to teach others also." 2 Timothy 2:2

3. Read 2 Corinthians 2:12–13, 7:5–7 to gain more insight into what Luke leaves out of Acts 20:1–4. What do you learn?

> Paul wrote 2 Corinthians during this time, approximately a year after writing 1 Corinthians.

> "This is the first clear reference in Scripture to Christians meeting to worship on the first day of the week rather than on the Sabbath, the seventh day. This coincides with Jesus' resurrection from the tomb on the first day of the week." (see Matthew 28:1, Mark 16:2) – from *The Expository Notes of Dr. Thomas Constable*, which are available online and free.

Empowered: The Amazing Church of Jesus Christ

4. Eutychus experienced the power and grace of God in a most memorable way. What happened? (Acts 20:10–12)

5. The death and revival of the boy—who was likely between eight to fourteen years old—was almost parenthetical in this account of Paul's teaching. Note that in verse 7, Paul is talking "to" the believers; in verse 11, he talked "with" them. How does faithful teaching and edifying discussion of Scripture strengthen the Church?

> This is Paul's final miracle in Acts.

6. What has Paul done in Acts 20 to make sure the believers and the Church will continue to grow after he is gone? In other words, how is Paul making disciples?

7. Use the map on page 146 to trace this final leg of Paul's third missionary journey. At this point, Paul was 610 miles from Jerusalem and five weeks away from Pentecost.

8. Use a dictionary to define *exhort/exhortation* and write the definition below.

9. What were some of Paul's exhortations in Scripture? Choose at least ONE and write it below:

Romans 6:11–13   Colossians 3:12–14
Galatians 6:1–5   Titus 2:7–8
Philippians 2:3–4

How could you apply that exhortation to your life this week?

Paul was as loving and compassionate as he was tenacious and resolved in this tender scene. His seaside speech summed up his heart and his purpose to the Ephesian church leaders and to us, with instructions as relevant today as they were then. The Holy Spirit was compelling Paul to go to Jerusalem—the center of the Jewish world where he'd once made his mark as a Pharisee of Pharisees, and from there to Rome—the foundation of wealth, politics, military force, and immorality in the Roman Empire. Few among us would willingly choose a path knowing suffering was assured. But Paul had no regard for his own safety. As a captive of Christ, his burden for the lost weighed more heavily on him than any bond that would restrain him.

---

17 From Miletus he sent to Ephesus and called to him the elders of the church. **18** And when they had come to him, he said to them,

"You yourselves know, from the first day that I set foot in Asia, how I was with you the whole time, **19** serving the Lord with all humility and with tears and with trials which came upon me through the plots of the Jews; **20** how I did not shrink from declaring to you anything that was profitable, and teaching you publicly and from house to house, **21** solemnly testifying to both Jews and Greeks of repentance toward God and faith in our Lord Jesus Christ. **22** And now, behold, bound by the Spirit, I am on my way to Jerusalem, not knowing what will happen to me there, **23** except that the Holy Spirit solemnly testifies to me in every city, saying that bonds and afflictions await me. **24** But I do not consider my life of any account as dear to myself, so that I may finish my course and the ministry which I received from the Lord Jesus, to testify solemnly of the gospel of the grace of God.

25 "And now, behold, I know that all of you, among whom I went about preaching the kingdom, will no longer see my face. **26** Therefore, I testify to you this day that I am innocent of the blood of all men. **27** For I did not shrink from declaring to you the whole purpose of God. **28** Be on guard for yourselves and for all the flock, among which the Holy Spirit has made you overseers, to shepherd the church of God which He purchased with His own blood. **29** I know that after my departure savage wolves will come in among you, not sparing the flock; **30** and from among your own selves men will arise, speaking perverse things, to draw away the disciples after them. **31** Therefore be on the alert, remembering that night and day for a period of three years I did not cease to admonish each one with tears. **32** And now I commend you to God and to the word of His grace, which is able to build you up and to give you the inheritance among all those who are sanctified. **33** I have coveted no one's silver or gold or clothes. **34** You yourselves know that these hands ministered to my own needs and to the men who were with me. **35** In everything I showed you that by working hard in this manner you must help the weak and remember the words of the Lord Jesus, that He Himself said, 'It is more blessed to give than to receive.'"

36 When he had said these things, he knelt down and prayed with them all.

37 And they began to weep aloud and embraced Paul, and repeatedly kissed him, **38** grieving especially over the word which he had spoken, that they would not see his face again. And they were accompanying him to the ship.

---

1. Paul did not establish the church in Ephesus (see Acts 18:18–21), but what did he do to help provide its structure and leadership? (Acts 20:17)

> Miletus was thirty miles from Ephesus. It was a day's journey there and another day of travel to return. Gathering this group could have taken up to four days.

2. How does Paul describe his ministry to them in verses 18b–19? What adjectives would you use to describe Paul's ministry in Asia?

> Paul's ministry in Ephesus lasted for three years.

3. What did the Holy Spirit testify to Paul in verse 23?

4. How does Paul respond to that unsettling promise in verse 24?

5. What do followers in Christ have in common with Paul?

   Psalm 34:19

   John 16:33

   1 Peter 2:21

6. Paul knew these would be his last words to this church this side of heaven (Acts 20:25) and declared himself "innocent of the blood of all men" in verse 26. How does verse 27 explain why he is innocent?

7. What warnings does Paul give these church leaders in verses 28–31?

8. How does Paul encourage the church to carry on in his absence? (Acts 20:32)

9. How does Paul describe the example he set for the family of God in Acts 20:34–35?

 10. Describe the emotional scene in verses 36–38 in your own words. How do you know Paul loved and was loved by these people to whom he had brought the message of the Gospel?

> The words used to describe their sorrow in these verses refer to a graphic experience of emotional pain. It is the same word used in Luke 2:48 when Mary and Joseph frantically searched for their lost son, Jesus.

A DEEPER LOOK

Paul never saw his Ephesian brothers and sisters in Christ again, but they do show up once more in Scripture (in addition to the letter Paul wrote them).

Read Revelation 2:1–5. According to this passage:

How did the church in Ephesus fulfill the charge Paul gave the elders on the beach at Miletus?

STUDY FIVE | Acts 21:1–16
Submitted to Suffering

Paul's third missionary journey ends here. And before he made his way to Jerusalem, he experienced God's kindness at every turn. The hospitality of an old friend and divine preparation from a familiar prophet gave Paul the strength and support he needed to move forward. Paul was surrounded by concern and was even begged to reconsider. Paul had a choice, after all, but he wasn't interested in an easy way out. He was ready to face whatever lay ahead, for the glory of God and the advancement of the Gospel. Like Jesus' humble prayer in the Garden, these disciples also submitted their will to God, walking alongside their friend as he followed in the footsteps of the Savior.

1 When we had parted from them and had set sail, we ran a straight course to Cos and the next day to Rhodes and from there to Patara; **2** and having found a ship crossing over to Phoenicia, we went aboard and set sail. **3** When we came in sight of Cyprus, leaving it on the left, we kept sailing to Syria and landed at Tyre; for there the ship was to unload its cargo. **4** After looking up the disciples, we stayed there seven days; and they kept telling Paul through the Spirit not to set foot in Jerusalem. **5** When our days there were ended, we left and started on our journey, while they all, with wives and children, escorted us until we were out of the city. After kneeling down on the beach and praying, we said farewell to one another. **6** Then we went on board the ship, and they returned home again.

7 When we had finished the voyage from Tyre, we arrived at Ptolemais, and after greeting the brethren, we stayed with them for a day. **8** On the next day we left and came to Caesarea, and entering the house of Philip the evangelist, who was one of the seven, we stayed with him. **9** Now this man had four virgin daughters who were prophetesses. **10** As we were staying there for some days, a prophet named Agabus came down from Judea. **11** And coming to us, he took Paul's belt and bound his own feet and hands, and said, "This is what the Holy Spirit says: 'In this way the Jews at Jerusalem will bind the man who owns this belt and deliver him into the hands of the Gentiles.'" **12** When we had heard this, we as well as the local residents began begging him not to go up to Jerusalem. **13** Then Paul answered, "What are you doing, weeping and breaking my heart? For I am ready not only to be bound, but even to die at Jerusalem for the name of the Lord Jesus." **14** And since he would not be persuaded, we fell silent, remarking, "The will of the Lord be done!"

15 After these days we got ready and started on our way up to Jerusalem. **16** Some of the disciples from Caesarea also came with us, taking us to Mnason of Cyprus, a disciple of long standing with whom we were to lodge.

---

1. After Paul's heart wrenching departure from the Ephesians, he and his companions sailed along the Asian coastline, then boarded a larger ship and travelled 400 miles across open water to Tyre.

   What did Paul do when he arrived and what was he repeatedly told by the disciples? (v. 4)

2. Paul spent just one week in Tyre, but what does the familiar scene in verses 5−6 indicate about the impact of his ministry on the believers there?

3. Where did Paul go next and who did he and his companions lodge with? What do we learn about this man and his family? (vv.8–9)

4. A prophet named Agabus delivered a message to Paul while he was in Tyre. What was his prophesy concerning Paul's future? (vv.10–11)

5. Who else heard the message and how did they respond? (v. 12)

6. How did Paul feel about their reaction to the prophecy and what was his resolve? (v. 13)

7. How did the past assurances Paul received from the Lord help prepare him for these current conversations?

Acts 19:21

Acts 20:22–24

8. What distracts you most from following God and His purposes for your life? How can you keep your focus on God's leading, regardless of your emotions or circumstances?

A DEEPER LOOK

Paul was faithful not only in his calling to spread the Gospel of Jesus Christ, but in his willingness to continually give up everything for the sake of Christ. Read the verses below that echo his attitude of humility, then answer the question that follows.

Galatians 2:20
Philippians 1:21

How does Paul's attitude about his life encourage, convict, or challenge you?

WEEK 10 TEACHING NOTES

Empowered: The Amazing Church of Jesus Christ

Week 10

Acts 21:17–23:35

"Away With Him!"

For ten years, Paul was freely on the move, preaching the Gospel to everyone he encountered and turning the world upside down as he went. Paul's Spirit-directed, faithful ministry advanced the Church and the message of grace beyond human boundaries and geographical borders, from Antioch to Athens and everywhere in between.

In this passage—true to his words on the shores of Miletus—Paul reached Jerusalem. He reconnected with brothers he hadn't seen since his faith and reputation were still new, and they marveled together at the work of God. Paul's zeal for God's mission was matched only by the unrelenting hostility of the Jews, who had their own agenda to carry out. Paul began his journey "bound in the Spirit to go to Jerusalem" but, once he arrived, it only took a few days for his persecutors to have him bound in chains.

The means and method of Paul's ministry will change in the last seven chapters of Acts. His movements will be restricted by the law of the land and the schemes of man. But the Gospel knows no such bounds. Even in bleak circumstances, this shackled servant made the Savior known, testifying to captors and adversaries about the freedom he found in God's amazing grace.

KEY VERSE:

"But on the night immediately following, the Lord stood at his side and said, 'Take courage; for as you have solemnly witnessed to My cause at Jerusalem, so you must witness at Rome also.'"

ACTS 23:11

STUDY ONE | Acts 21:17–36
Paul Arrives in Jerusalem

Some consider this final section of Acts to be Paul's fourth missionary journey. It will include only three cities and a seemingly more limited audience, but it will be the culmination of the promises and prophecy spoken over Paul the day he opened his heart to his Messiah. When he arrived in Jerusalem, Paul united with Church leadership to share beautiful details of the work done in Jesus' name. The tension discussed among these brothers set the tone for Paul's time in Jerusalem. The body of Christ was growing, but there were still obstacles to overcome and bridges to build. And Paul demonstrated he was willing to "endure all things so that we will cause no hindrance to the gospel of Christ." (1 Corinthians 9:12)

---

17 After we arrived in Jerusalem, the brethren received us gladly. **18** And the following day Paul went in with us to James, and all the elders were present. **19** After he had greeted them, he began to relate one by one the things which God had done among the Gentiles through his ministry. **20** And when they heard it they began glorifying God; and they said to him, "You see, brother, how many thousands there are among the Jews of those who have believed, and they are all zealous for the Law; **21** and they have been told about you, that you are teaching all the Jews who are among the Gentiles to forsake Moses, telling them not to circumcise their children nor to walk according to the customs. **22** What, then, is to be done? They will certainly hear that you have come. **23** Therefore do this that we tell you. We have four men who are under a vow; **24** take them and purify yourself along with them, and pay their expenses so that they may shave their heads; and all will know that there is nothing to the things which they have been told about you, but that you yourself also walk orderly, keeping the Law. **25** But concerning the Gentiles who have believed, we wrote, having decided that they should abstain from meat sacrificed to idols and from blood and from what is strangled and from fornication." **26** Then Paul took the men, and the next day, purifying himself along with them, went into the temple giving notice of the completion of the days of purification, until the sacrifice was offered for each one of them.

27 When the seven days were almost over, the Jews from Asia, upon seeing him in the temple, began to stir up all the crowd and laid hands on him, **28** crying out, "Men of Israel, come to our aid! This is the man who preaches to all men everywhere against our people and the Law and this place; and besides he has even brought Greeks into the temple and has defiled this holy place." **29** For they had previously seen Trophimus the Ephesian in the city with him, and they supposed that Paul had brought him into the temple. **30** Then all the city was provoked, and the people rushed together, and taking hold of Paul they dragged him out of the temple, and immediately the doors were shut. **31** While they were seeking to kill him, a report came up to the commander of the Roman cohort that all Jerusalem was in confusion. **32** At once he took along some soldiers and centurions and ran down to them; and when they saw the commander and the soldiers, they stopped beating Paul. **33** Then the commander came up and took hold of him, and ordered him to be bound with two chains; and he began asking who he was and what he had done. **34** But among the crowd some were shouting one thing and some another, and when he could not find out the facts because of the uproar, he ordered him to be brought into the barracks. **35** When he got to the stairs, he was carried by the soldiers because of the violence of the mob; **36** for the multitude of the people kept following them, shouting, "Away with him!"

---

1. In Acts 21:18–19 Paul spent time with James and the elders. What did they discuss? Why is it important to remember and share with other believers the work of God in your life?

2. What was important for Paul to know about the group of believers in Jerusalem? (vv. 20–21)

3. What were the Christian leaders concerned about and what strategy did the elders offer to help combat the false rumors about Paul and his teaching? (vv. 22–24)

4. How did Paul attempt to remove doubt about his commitment to his Jewish heritage in Acts 21:26? Read 1 Corinthians 9:19–22 below for further insight.

   "For though I am free from all men, I have made myself a slave to all, so that I may win more. To the Jews I became as a Jew, so that I might win Jews; to those who are under the Law, as under the Law though not being myself under the Law, so that I might win those who are under the Law; to those who are without law, as without law, though not being without the law of God but under the law of Christ, so that I might win those who are without law. To the weak I became weak, that I might win the weak; I have become all things to all men, so that I may by all means save some."

5. In Acts 21:27 some Jews from Asia recognized Paul in the temple and reacted in anger. What did they accuse him of and what assumption did they make? (vv. 28–29)

James, who wrote the book of James, was the half-brother of Jesus. He was one of the key leaders of the Church at the time.

Scholars estimate there were as many as 25,000–50,000 believing Jews in Jerusalem at this time.

"The Nazirite vow is taken by individuals who have voluntarily dedicated themselves to God. The vow is a decision, action, and desire on the part of people whose desire is to yield themselves to God completely. By definition, the Hebrew word *nazir* simply means "to be separated or consecrated." The Nazirite vow, which appears in Numbers 6:1–21, has five features. It is voluntary, can be done by either men or women, has a specific time frame, has specific requirements and restrictions, and at its conclusion a sacrifice is offered." From *gotquestions.com*

"Paul's cleansing would be necessary because of his travels in "unclean" Gentile territory. This act would represent a conciliatory gesture. Paul would have supported a "law-free" mission to the Gentiles as an option, but this gesture would represent an attempt to be sensitive to the Jews." note from the *NET Bible*

"Gentiles were not allowed into the main temple area. Four-and-a-half-foot tall stone markers inscribed in Greek and Latin in the outer court that surrounded the Court of Women announced to foreigners that they were prohibited from entering the sanctuary." From the *Baker Exegetical Commentary on the New Testament*, Dr. Darrell Bock

6. Who did the Lord send to intervene in this dangerous situation? (vv. 31b–33)

7. What prophecy is fulfilled in verse 33? (See Acts 21:10–11)

8. How did this situation continue to escalate? (Acts 21:34–36)

> All of Jerusalem was provoked by the events in Acts 21:30–31. The language used here paints a picture of people running from all parts of the city to form a mob. The verbs used ("taking hold" and "dragged") depict sudden and repetitive forced movement— violent action against Paul by an enraged and confused mass of people.

9. What other time in Scripture have we seen an irrational, bloodthirsty crowd in Jerusalem seek to harm the one sent with the message of truth and hope?

"But they cried out all together, saying, 'Away with this man, and release for us Barabbas!' (He was one who had been thrown into prison for an insurrection made in the city, and for murder.) Pilate, wanting to release Jesus, addressed them again, but they kept on calling out, saying, 'Crucify, crucify Him!' And he said to them the third time, 'Why, what evil has this man done? I have found in Him no guilt demanding death; therefore I will punish Him and release Him.' But they were insistent, with loud voices asking that He be crucified. And their voices began to prevail. And Pilate pronounced sentence that their demand be granted." Luke 23:18–24

A DEEPER LOOK

Can you think of any non-essential spiritual issues about which believers can show greater sensitivity toward one another? Some examples include political preference, worship style, or style of church governance.

How can your expression of freedom be a hindrance to the Gospel for someone else?

What could you do to promote unity without compromising the Gospel?

STUDY TWO | Acts 21:37–22:21
Paul Testifies to the Jerusalem Jews

Picture Paul standing in chains giving this defense. His voice filled the air as he gestured with passion, the quiet interrupted only by the rattle of iron that was binding his hands and feet. Clenched fists among the crowd revealed the Jews' rage was unabated, and Paul understood. It wasn't that long ago that he would have been the one stirring up their fury but, after he encountered the living Lord, Paul was undone and made new. This mob was ready to annihilate the man and his message, but Paul—just a few steps from safety—stopped to share his story of transformation, praying their eyes would finally see.

---

37 As Paul was about to be brought into the barracks, he said to the commander, "May I say something to you?" And he said, "Do you know Greek? **38** Then you are not the Egyptian who some time ago stirred up a revolt and led the four thousand men of the Assassins out into the wilderness?" **39** But Paul said, "I am a Jew of Tarsus in Cilicia, a citizen of no insignificant city; and I beg you, allow me to speak to the people." **40** When he had given him permission, Paul, standing on the stairs, motioned to the people with his hand; and when there was a great hush, he spoke to them in the Hebrew dialect, saying,

22 "Brethren and fathers, hear my defense which I now offer to you."
2 And when they heard that he was addressing them in the Hebrew dialect, they became even more quiet; and he said,
3 "I am a Jew, born in Tarsus of Cilicia, but brought up in this city, educated under Gamaliel, strictly according to the law of our fathers, being zealous for God just as you all are today. **4** I persecuted this Way to the death, binding and putting both men and women into prisons, **5** as also the high priest and all the Council of the elders can testify. From them I also received letters to the brethren, and started off for Damascus in order to bring even those who were there to Jerusalem as prisoners to be punished.
6 "But it happened that as I was on my way, approaching Damascus about noontime, a very bright light suddenly flashed from heaven all around me, **7** and I fell to the ground and heard a voice saying to me, 'Saul, Saul, why are you persecuting Me?' **8** And I answered, 'Who are You, Lord?' And He said to me, 'I am Jesus the Nazarene, whom you are persecuting.' **9** And those who were with me saw the light, to be sure, but did not understand the voice of the

One who was speaking to me. **10** And I said, 'What shall I do, Lord?' And the Lord said to me, 'Get up and go on into Damascus, and there you will be told of all that has been appointed for you to do.' **11** But since I could not see because of the brightness of that light, I was led by the hand by those who were with me and came into Damascus.

12 "A certain Ananias, a man who was devout by the standard of the Law, and well spoken of by all the Jews who lived there, **13** came to me, and standing near said to me, 'Brother Saul, receive your sight!' And at that very time I looked up at him. **14** And he said, 'The God of our fathers has appointed you to know His will and to see the Righteous One and to hear an utterance from His mouth. **15** For you will be a witness for Him to all men of what you have seen and heard. **16** Now why do you delay? Get up and be baptized, and wash away your sins, calling on His name.'

17 "It happened when I returned to Jerusalem and was praying in the temple, that I fell into a trance, **18** and I saw Him saying to me, 'Make haste, and get out of Jerusalem quickly, because they will not accept your testimony about Me.' **19** And I said, 'Lord, they themselves understand that in one synagogue after another I used to imprison and beat those who believed in You. **20** And when the blood of Your witness Stephen was being shed, I also was standing by approving, and watching out for the coats of those who were slaying him.' **21** And He said to me, 'Go! For I will send you far away to the Gentiles.'"

---

1. What two things surprised the commander about Paul in verses 37–38?

> With several hundred thousand citizens, Tarsus was one of the great cities of the Roman empire on the southern coast of Asia Minor and an intellectual center of the day.

2. Who does Paul say he is and what was his request in verse 39?

3. What adjustment did Paul make in his speech before the Jews that encouraged them to listen? (vv. 21:40–22:2)

4. Paul chose to speak before a violent crowd that was seeking to take his life. How is Paul's willingness to share the Gospel with people who hated him a reflection of the heart and the grace of God?

Empowered: The Amazing Church of Jesus Christ

5. How did Paul describe his life before Christ in Acts 22:3–5?

6. Paul shares his conversion experience in verses 6–11. To "convert" means to change in form, character, or function. Conversion takes place not only in our hearts, but in our minds, missions, desires, goals, and purposes. As a child of God, along with your salvation, what has God "converted" in your life?

7. What insights did Ananias reveal to Paul and what significant promise did he make about Jesus? (vv. 12–16)

8. Paul received a warning and direction in verses 17–18. Who did Paul see and what was he told to do?

9. Paul objected in verses 19–20, based on his former life and the credibility he thought it would provide. What new calling did the Lord give to Paul in verse 21?

10. What do we learn and observe about God—His character and relationship with man—from Paul's testimony?

STUDY THREE | Acts 22:22–23:5
A Roman Citizen Revealed

With one word, the crowd became unhinged, and the Romans were at a loss. Following their baser instincts, the commander decided physical punishment would "inspire" Paul to reveal any hidden motives. But Paul shared a crucial detail with them at the last minute that prompted an immediate shift in treatment and tone. They then passed him off to the Council for interrogation, and this ironic move was surely not lost on Paul. This was the same group that gave him authority to arrest Christians in Damascus and anywhere else they were found. They claimed to love their Law, but these "super saints" broke more than a few commandments in their exchange with the former Pharisee. This wasn't the first time they'd come face-to-face with the truth, but hypocrisy by nature is blind. And these men had been given every chance to see the light.

---

22 They listened to him up to this statement, and then they raised their voices and said, "Away with such a fellow from the earth, for he should not be allowed to live!" **23** And as they were crying out and throwing off their cloaks and tossing dust into the air, **24** the commander ordered him to be brought into the barracks, stating that he should be examined by scourging so that he might find out the reason why they were shouting against him that way. **25** But when they stretched him out with thongs, Paul said to the centurion who was standing by, "Is it lawful for you to scourge a man who is a Roman and uncondemned?" **26** When the centurion heard this, he went to the commander and told him, saying, "What are you about to do? For this man is a Roman." **27** The commander came and said to him, "Tell me, are you a Roman?" And he said, "Yes." **28** The commander answered, "I acquired this citizenship with a large sum of money." And Paul said, "But I was actually born a citizen." **29** Therefore those who were about to examine him immediately let go of him; and the commander also was afraid when he found out that he was a Roman, and because he had put him in chains. **30** But on the next day, wishing to know for certain why he had been accused by the Jews, he released him and ordered the chief priests and all the Council to assemble, and brought Paul down and set him before them.

23 **1** Paul, looking intently at the Council, said, "Brethren, I have lived my life with a perfectly good conscience before God up to this day." **2** The high priest Ananias commanded those standing beside him to strike him on the mouth. **3** Then Paul said to him, "God is going to strike you, you whitewashed wall! Do you sit to try me according to the Law, and in violation of the Law order me to be struck?" **4** But the bystanders said, "Do you revile God's high priest?" **5** And Paul said, "I was not aware, brethren, that he was high priest; for it is written, 'You shall not speak evil of a ruler of your people.'"

---

1. In Acts 22:21 Paul shared his commission from God to share the Gospel with the Gentiles. How did the crowd respond? (vv. 22–23)

> The Greek word for "crying out" in verse 23 refers to the sound of screaming, like a dog barking or raven squawking.

Empowered: The Amazing Church of Jesus Christ

2. How does their attitude of rejection contradict their original mission as a nation? Look up the verses below for insight.

   Isaiah 49:6

   Isaiah 52:10

3. Why would Paul respond with the Law? Read Hebrews 4:12.

4. What was the purpose of the Roman commander's scourging in this intensely chaotic scene in Acts 22:24?

> "Scourging by the Roman flagellum (a wooden handle to which were attached leather thongs tipped with bits of metal and bone) was a fearful ordeal from which men frequently died (from loss of blood or infection). Jesus endured it before His crucifixion. Such a beating would have surpassed anything Paul had previously experienced. In preparation, the guards stretched him out with thongs to make his body taut and magnify the effects of the flagellation."
> John MacArthur, *The MacArthur New Testament Commentary*

5. Paul knew how to respond in the moment! Where was he in verse 25 and what important detail did he reveal about his background?

6. The Roman commander had violated Paul's rights as a Roman citizen; but he is still unsure why the Jews are so upset with Paul. What did he decide to do to get his questions answered? (v.30)

> "To bind a Roman citizen is a crime, to flog him an abomination, to slay him is almost an act of murder.' The officer paid a large sum of money to become a Roman citizen, usually in the form of a bribe. Paul's citizenship was passed down from his father, indicating his father may have had some social status."
> Darrell Bock, *Acts: Baker Exegetical Commentary on The New Testament*

7. How did the high priest respond in Acts 23:2 to Paul's honest self-evaluation in verse 1?

> This was the sixth time recorded in the Scripture that the Sanhedrin had met to consider the claims of Christ: John 11:47–53; Matthew 26:57–68; Acts 4:5–22; Acts 5:21–40; Acts 6:12–7:60

8. What was Paul unaware of in Acts 23:3–4?

9. What was Paul's posture in verse 5 when called out about his attitude toward the leader in the room?

10. How can we, as God's people, disagree but not disrespect those God has put in authority over us?

A DEEPER LOOK

In the opening scene in Acts 23, Paul was essentially rebuked for the disrespect he showed toward the high priest. Paul immediately responded in deference to the position of authority, a humble posture not often seen in the world today.

Choose and look up at least ONE verse to determine what the Bible says about the effect a godly rebuke, or reproof, can have on our hearts, and what happens when godly instruction is ignored:

Proverbs 5:12–14   Proverbs 13:18
Proverbs 6:23   Proverbs 15:31–32
Proverbs 10:17   Proverbs 19:20

STUDY | **Acts 23:6–22**
FOUR | **A Conspiracy Unraveled**

After an exhausting day filled with conflict on every side, Paul must've welcomed the darkness. But the heavenly Father knew His child was weary and unsettled, so He spoke words of life and hope into Paul's soul. After a night spent resting in the Lord's presence, the sun rose on another plot against him. A familiar group filled with hatred set out to destroy God's faithful servant, even putting their own lives down as "collateral." But a sovereignly placed "secret weapon" was in the right place at the right time—something the world calls a "coincidence"—and shared what he overheard with those who could keep Paul safe.

---

6 But perceiving that one group were Sadducees and the other Pharisees, Paul began crying out in the Council, "Brethren, I am a Pharisee, a son of Pharisees; I am on trial for the hope and resurrection of the dead!" **7** As he said this, there occurred a dissension between the Pharisees and Sadducees, and the assembly was divided. **8** For the Sadducees say that there is no resurrection, nor an angel, nor a spirit, but the Pharisees acknowledge them all. **9** And there occurred a great uproar; and some of the scribes of the Pharisaic party stood up and began to argue heatedly, saying, "We find nothing wrong with this man; suppose a spirit or an angel has spoken to him?" **10** And as a great dissension was developing, the commander was afraid Paul would be torn to pieces by them and ordered the troops to go down and take him away from them by force, and bring him into the barracks.

11 But on the night immediately following, the Lord stood at his side and said, "Take courage; for as you have solemnly witnessed to My cause at Jerusalem, so you must witness at Rome also."

12 When it was day, the Jews formed a conspiracy and bound themselves under an oath, saying that they would neither eat nor drink until they had killed Paul. **13** There were more than forty who formed this plot. **14** They came to the chief priests and the elders and said, "We have bound ourselves under a solemn oath to taste nothing until we have killed Paul. **15** Now therefore, you and the Council notify the commander to bring him down to you, as though you were going to determine his case by a more thorough investigation; and we for our part are ready to slay him before he comes near the place."

16 But the son of Paul's sister heard of their ambush, and he came and entered the barracks and told Paul. **17** Paul called one of the centurions to him and said, "Lead this young man to the commander, for he has something to report to him." **18** So he took him and led him to the commander and said, "Paul the prisoner called me to him and asked me to lead this young man to you since he has something to tell you." **19** The commander took him by the hand and stepping aside, began to inquire of him privately, "What is it that you have to report to me?" **20** And he said, "The Jews have agreed to ask you to bring Paul down tomorrow to the Council, as though they were going to inquire somewhat more thoroughly about him. **21** So do not listen to them, for more than forty of them are lying in wait for him who have bound themselves under a curse not to eat or drink until they slay him; and now they are ready and waiting for the promise from you." **22** So the commander let the young man go, instructing him, "Tell no one that you have notified me of these things."

---

1. Paul notices that he is speaking to Sadducees and Pharisees in verse 6. Paul also finally declares why he was on trial (see Acts 22:30) in Acts 23:6. This caused an argument among the assembly. (v. 7)

   Why was Paul's statement so controversial, according to verse 8?

> "Pharisees strictly adhere to the Law with extensive rules and traditions to maintain the integrity of it. Sadducees, a Jewish sect who did not believe in the traditions, but only the Law. As such they do not believe in resurrection, spirits, or angels." from *The Lexham Bible Dictionary*

2. Their disagreement digressed into mayhem (v. 9) and Paul's life was in danger once more. How did his Roman guards respond? (v.10)

3. The Lord comes to Paul in prison. What hope did He provide Paul? (v. 11)

4. How does God's Word guide your thinking in times of fear and doubt? Choose and look up at least ONE verse below to memorize and meditate on in anxious times, then write your verse in the space below.

Psalm 31:24   1 Corinthians 16:13
Psalm 56:3–4   2 Timothy 1:7
Isaiah 41:10   1 John 4:18

5. The Lord provided Paul with an eternal perspective. Read the passage below; how does it describe eternity's view of our service for the sake of Christ and the Gospel?

"Therefore, my beloved brethren, be steadfast, immovable, always abounding in the work of the Lord, knowing that your toil is not in vain in the Lord." 1 Corinthians 15:58

6. The enraged Jews decided to organize in Acts 23:12–15. Describe their plans and the lengths they would go to stop Paul.

> In Hebrew the word for "vow" is *cherem*. Taking such a vow is saying, in essence, "May God curse me if I fail to do this!"

7. The Jews' perfect plan was thwarted by an unlikely character. What happened in verse 16?

> Paul's nephew was able to see Paul because Roman prisoners were allowed to have visitors such as family and friends who could provide them with food and other necessities.

A DEEPER LOOK

Verses 16–22 are an example of the providence of God at work in Paul's life. Baker's *Evangelical Dictionary of Biblical Theology* defines *providence* this way:

"Providence ... is the sovereign, divine superintendence of all things, guiding them toward their divinely predetermined end in a way that is consistent with their created nature, all to the glory and praise of God."

In other words, nothing happens by chance, coincidence, or accident. God uses every piece and part of His creation to work His will and perfect purposes in our lives and in the world, for His glory.

How does Scripture talk about God's providence?

Genesis 50:19–20   Lamentations 3:37–38
Proverbs 16:4, 9   Amos 3:6

Share a time you witnessed the providence of God. What did you learn about His purposes and heart?

STUDY FIVE | Acts 23:23–35 | From Jerusalem to Caesarea

The big picture behind this story is that Paul was moving toward Rome, and he was assured that suffering and chains would be part of the journey. That difficult promise would be enough to make most people shrink back. But while Paul was hard-pressed on every side, God did not forsake him—and He often displayed His power in the details. The seemingly small decisions made by violent mobs and godless men were, in reality, God's protection and provision. The most mundane matters were actually the tracks that moved God's servant and His message further along in eternity's greater purposes.

---

23 And he called to him two of the centurions and said, "Get two hundred soldiers ready by the third hour of the night to proceed to Caesarea, with seventy horsemen and two hundred spearmen." **24** They were also to provide mounts to put Paul on and bring him safely to Felix the governor. **25** And he wrote a letter having this form:

26 "Claudius Lysias, to the most excellent governor Felix, greetings.
27 "When this man was arrested by the Jews and was about to be slain by them, I came up to them with the troops and rescued him, having learned that he was a Roman. **28** "And wanting to ascertain the charge for which they were accusing him, I brought him down to their Council; **29** and I found him to be accused over questions about their Law, but under no accusation deserving death or imprisonment.
30 "When I was informed that there would be a plot against the man, I sent him to you at once, also instructing his accusers to bring charges against him before you."
31 So the soldiers, in accordance with their orders, took Paul and brought him by night to Antipatris. **32** But the next day, leaving the horsemen to go

on with him, they returned to the barracks. 33 When these had come to Caesarea and delivered the letter to the governor, they also presented Paul to him. **34** When he had read it, he asked from what province he was, and when he learned that he was from Cilicia, **35** he said, "I will give you a hearing after your accusers arrive also," giving orders for him to be kept in Herod's Praetorium.

---

1. What action did the commander take in response to the report from Paul's nephew? (vv. 23–24)

The third hour of the night is 9 p.m.

2. In addition to the escorts, what did the commander send with Paul? (v. 25)

3. Why did the Roman commander, Claudius Lysias, alter the events recorded in his letter to Felix? (See Acts 22:25–29)

Marcus Antonius Felix was the successor of Pontius Pilate and governor in Judea for five years. He was born a slave and, through his brother, won the favor of Claudius Caesar. He was the first slave in history to become governor of a Roman province. The Roman historian Tacitus tells us Felix was a cruel ruler and crucified many rebels. It was said that he "wielded the power of a king with the mind of a slave."

4. According to Acts 23:30, who else will be meeting with Felix the governor in Caesarea?

5. Based on the content of Claudius Lysias' letter, should Paul still be in custody?

Based on Jesus' prophetic words below in Mark 13:9, why do you think he was?

"But be on your guard; for they will deliver you to the courts, and you will be flogged in the synagogues, and you will stand before governors and kings for My sake, as a testimony to them."

6. After Felix confirmed Paul was from his jurisdiction and that he was responsible for trying the case (v. 34), where did he send Paul? (v. 35)

> Cilicia was an imperial province under direct control of the emperor at the time. Herod's Praetorium was the lavish palace built by Herod the Great and served as the capitol building as well as the official residence of the Roman governor.

 7. Where do you see God's grace and protection over Paul in this passage as he moves closer to Rome?

8. Paul was moving forward in his journey but, rather than as a free man, he was in chains and under guard. Without the background and understanding we have from the context of God's Word, it would appear Paul's plans have been derailed.

Does a situation in your life right now feel similarly "out of control?" Are there circumstances in which it seems God is not at work or has forgotten about you? With the hope in God's providence and sovereignty in view, what encouragement do you find in this passage?

WEEK 11 TEACHING NOTES

Empowered: The Amazing Church of Jesus Christ

Acts 24–26

Kept in Custody in Caesarea

As we walk with Paul this week through a prison, a praetorium, and a palace, we see many predictions for his ministry come to pass. He had preached to Jews in the synagogues and Gentiles in the square; now he would give his testimony before high priests, a governor, and a king.

Paul was accustomed to and prepared for persecution. He'd presented the gift of grace to thousands, and many accepted with joy. But he'd also received beatings and captivity in return. This week, we see Paul facing some of his most difficult moments, enduring baseless accusations and unreasonable imprisonment. But God still received all the glory as His servant, once again, strategically shared his conversion story—a picture of new life emerging from old roots.

Paul's season in Caesarea resulted in the fulfillment of prophecy and placed him in position to make the ultimate sacrifice. And he held fast to his profession from Acts 21:13: "I am ready" to do anything "for the name of the Lord Jesus." Like his Savior when He stood before Pilate, Paul was innocent yet accused and in chains. But he bore the shackles gladly, if it meant that everyone within the sound of his voice would hear of redemption and receive life.

KEY VERSE:

"So, having obtained help from God, I stand to this day testifying both to small and great, stating nothing but what the Prophets and Moses said was going to take place; that the Christ was to suffer, and that by reason of His resurrection from the dead He would be the first to proclaim light both to the Jewish people and to the Gentiles."

ACTS 26:22–23

STUDY ONE | Acts 24:1–27
Paul before Felix

Tertullus was the original spin doctor. Like a spider weaving its web, he expertly twisted the words and actions of a man of God into a sticky trap, hoping to convince the powers that be to end Paul's life and thus stop the spreading "plague" of Christianity. But, thanks to a leader who preferred to stall rather than resolve, Paul was kept in custody instead, free to continue moving hearts toward Christ. While the religious and governing leaders used Paul like a pawn in their political game, in reality, God's sovereignty was orchestrating every event. And each interaction was a means to proclaim the truth and hope of Jesus.

---

1 After five days the high priest Ananias came down with some elders, with an attorney named Tertullus, and they brought charges to the governor against Paul. **2** After Paul had been summoned, Tertullus began to accuse him, saying to the governor,

"Since we have through you attained much peace, and since by your providence reforms are being carried out for this nation, **3** we acknowledge this in every way and everywhere, most excellent Felix, with all thankfulness. **4** But, that I may not weary you any further, I beg you to grant us, by your kindness, a brief hearing. **5** For we have found this man a real pest and a fellow who stirs up dissension among all the Jews throughout the world, and a ringleader of the sect of the Nazarenes. **6** And he even tried to desecrate the temple; and then we arrested him. [We wanted to judge him according to our own Law. **7** But Lysias the commander came along, and with much violence took him out of our hands, **8** ordering his accusers to come before you.] By examining him yourself concerning all these matters you will be able to ascertain the things of which we accuse him." **9** The Jews also joined in the attack, asserting that these things were so. **10** When the governor had nodded for him to speak, Paul responded:

"Knowing that for many years you have been a judge to this nation, I cheerfully make my defense, **11** since you can take note of the fact that no more than twelve days ago I went up to Jerusalem to worship. **12** Neither in the temple, nor in the synagogues, nor in the city itself did they find me carrying on a discussion with anyone or causing a riot. **13** Nor can they prove to you the charges of which they now accuse me. **14** But this I admit to you, that according to the Way which they call a sect I do serve the God of our fathers, believing everything that is in accordance with the Law and that is written in the Prophets; **15** having a hope in God, which these men cherish themselves, that there shall certainly be a resurrection of both the righteous and the wicked. **16** In view of this, I also do my best to maintain always a blameless conscience both before God and before men. **17** Now after several years I came to bring alms to my nation and to present offerings; **18** in which they found me occupied in the temple, having been purified, without any crowd or uproar. But there were some Jews from Asia— **19** who ought to have been present before you and to make accusation, if they should have anything against me. **20** Or else let these men themselves tell what misdeed they found when I stood before the Council, **21** other than for this one statement which I shouted out while standing among them, 'For the resurrection of the dead I am on trial before you today.'" **22** But Felix, having a more exact knowledge about the Way, put them off, saying, "When Lysias the commander comes down, I will decide your case." **23** Then he gave orders to the centurion for him to be kept

Empowered: The Amazing Church of Jesus Christ

in custody and yet have some freedom, and not to prevent any of his friends from ministering to him.

24 But some days later Felix arrived with Drusilla, his wife who was a Jewess, and sent for Paul and heard him speak about faith in Christ Jesus. **25** But as he was discussing righteousness, self-control and the judgment to come, Felix became frightened and said, "Go away for the present, and when I find time I will summon you." **26** At the same time too, he was hoping that money would be given him by Paul; therefore he also used to send for him quite often and converse with him. **27** But after two years had passed, Felix was succeeded by Porcius Festus, and wishing to do the Jews a favor, Felix left Paul imprisoned.

---

1. There are several moving parts in the next few verses. Let's orient ourselves first:

   Where had Paul been for five days? (Acts 23:33, 35)

   > Tertullus was a professional Gentile lawyer likely hired by the religious leaders to more persuasively present their case.

   Who "came down" and why? (Acts 24:1)

   Who was the audience for this hearing in verse 1? (first named in Acts 23:24)

2. Observe Paul's opening remarks in verse 10. How do they compare with the lawyer's words? Read Jesus' words below and note the blessing and hope they infuse into this scene.

   "When they bring you before the synagogues and the rulers and the authorities, do not worry about how or what you are to speak in your defense, or what you are to say; for the Holy Spirit will teach you in that very hour what you ought to say." Luke 12:11–12

3. Read through this passage depicting this courtroom scene. Record the charges levied and Paul's response to each in the chart on the next page.

Tertullus' accusation (v. 5a):	Paul's response (vv. 11–13):
Tertullus' accusation (v. 5b):	**Paul's response (vv. 14–16):**
Tertullus' accusation (v. 6):	**Paul's response (vv. 17–19*):**

*Verses 18–19 reference events from Acts 21:23–26 and Acts 23:1–10

 4. In Acts 24:21, Paul reiterates the reason for his persecution by the Jews. This is consistent with Paul's statements in Acts 23:6 and Acts 24:15. What was the reason and why was this such a "hot button issue" for the Jews?

5. What interesting note are we given about Felix and what decision did he make about the case against Paul? (Acts 24:22)

Empowered: The Amazing Church of Jesus Christ

6. How does God provide for Paul during this time? (v. 23)

7. How did Felix respond to Paul's teaching and what insight are we given into Felix's character? (vv. 24–26)

A DEEPER LOOK

The high priest Ananias and his consuming grudge. The Sanhedrin elders and their faulty theology. The hard-hearted ruler Felix and his foolish wife. Each character in this chapter clearly reveals that neither a strict adherence to the law, nor a knowledge of Christian teachings, nor even a long familiarity with the source of truth have any power to change a person's heart. Repentance, humility, the blood of Christ, and the power of the Holy Spirit are the only means by which we are transformed from God's hostile enemies (Colossians 1:21) into His beloved children (1 John 3:1).

Many opportunities to turn toward Christ were offered to the men and women in this passage, but they went unheeded. Choose at least ONE of the verses below and determine: what is the right response to the Holy Spirit's conviction of sin?

Psalm 32:1–7   Acts 2:38
Psalm 51:4   2 Corinthians 7:9–10
Proverbs 28:13–14   1 John 1:9

Titus 3:3–7 contains a beautiful encapsulation of who we were before Christ, how our Savior has powerfully worked on our behalf, and what our current and future hope is as His children. Read these verses then write them below.

STUDY TWO | Acts 25:1–12
Paul's Defense before Festus

The chess board pieces continued to move as new leadership came to power, bringing Paul and his accusers to the forefront once again. Despite the passage of time, the religious leaders remained entrenched in their hatred of Paul. And Paul was equally undeterred in his resolve to clear his name and continue the mission. The paradox of physics comes to mind here: what happens when an immovable object meets an unstoppable force? In this case, the hard-hearted Jews were coming up against the God of Job 23:13–14 (ESV), which makes the answer crystal clear: "But he is unchangeable, and who can turn him back? What he desires, that he does. For he will complete what he appoints for me, and many such things are in his mind."

---

1 Festus then, having arrived in the province, three days later went up to Jerusalem from Caesarea. **2** And the chief priests and the leading men of the Jews brought charges against Paul, and they were urging him, **3** requesting a concession against Paul, that he might have him brought to Jerusalem (at the same time, setting an ambush to kill him on the way). **4** Festus then answered that Paul was being kept in custody at Caesarea and that he himself was about to leave shortly. **5** "Therefore," he said, "let the influential men among you go there with me, and if there is anything wrong about the man, let them prosecute him."

6 After he had spent not more than eight or ten days among them, he went down to Caesarea, and on the next day he took his seat on the tribunal and ordered Paul to be brought. **7** After Paul arrived, the Jews who had come down from Jerusalem stood around him, bringing many and serious charges against him which they could not prove, **8** while Paul said in his own defense, "I have committed no offense either against the Law of the Jews or against the temple or against Caesar." **9** But Festus, wishing to do the Jews a favor, answered Paul and said, "Are you willing to go up to Jerusalem and stand trial before me on these charges?" **10** But Paul said, "I am standing before Caesar's tribunal, where I ought to be tried. I have done no wrong to the Jews, as you also very well know. **11** If, then, I am a wrongdoer and have committed anything worthy of death, I do not refuse to die; but if none of those things is true of which these men accuse me, no one can hand me over to them. I appeal to Caesar." **12** Then when Festus had conferred with his council, he answered, "You have appealed to Caesar, to Caesar you shall go."

---

1. What issue arose as soon as the new governor entered Jerusalem? (vv. 1–3a)

2. What is the underlying motive for their interest in Paul's relocation? (v. 3b)

Not only had Porcius Festus replaced Felix as the Roman governor of Judea (around 55–60 A.D.), Ananias had also been replaced by a new high priest named Ishmael. The historian Josephus records that Festus had a reputation for being kind to the Jews. He died in office after only two years.

Empowered: The Amazing Church of Jesus Christ

3. How did Festus unintentionally save Paul's life in verses 4–5?

4. Festus returns to Caesarea and the trial at last resumes. (vv. 6–7) How do the verses below provide commentary on the spiritual warfare taking place?

"This is the judgment, that the Light has come into the world, and men loved the darkness rather than the Light, for their deeds were evil. For everyone who does evil hates the Light, and does not come to the Light for fear that his deeds will be exposed. But he who practices the truth comes to the Light, so that his deeds may be manifested as having been wrought in God." John 3:19–21

5. What is Paul's defense in Acts 25:8? Based on verse 7, what should have been Festus' response? How do we know Festus cared more about politics and power than justice? (v. 9)

6. Read 1 Peter 3:13–17 below. How do we see this played out in Paul's life in Acts 25:8–11?

"Who is there to harm you if you prove zealous for what is good? But even if you should suffer for the sake of righteousness, you are blessed. And do not fear their intimidation, and do not be troubled, but sanctify Christ as Lord in your hearts, always being ready to make a defense to everyone who asks you to give an account for the hope that is in you, yet with gentleness and reverence; and keep a good conscience so that in the thing in which you are slandered, those who revile your good behavior in Christ will be put to shame. For it is better, if God should will it so, that you suffer for doing what is right rather than for doing what is wrong."

7. Acts 25:10–11 reveal Paul was prepared to move up the chain of command, and that meant the stakes were higher than ever before. Jesus' words in Luke 12:4–7 would have provided great comfort. Read the passage and record the reasons for Paul's confidence and courage.

"I say to you, My friends, do not be afraid of those who kill the body and after that have no more that they can do. But I will warn you whom to fear: fear the One who, after He has killed, has authority to cast into hell; yes, I tell you, fear Him! Are not five sparrows sold for two cents? Yet not one of them is forgotten before God. Indeed, the very hairs of your head are all numbered. Do not fear; you are more valuable than many sparrows."

8. What did Paul finally request at the end of Acts 25:11?

9. How does this fulfill Paul's commission from Acts 9:15: "But the Lord said to him, 'Go, for he is a chosen instrument of Mine, to bear My name before the Gentiles and kings and the sons of Israel...'"?

"It was the right of every Roman citizen to have his case heard by Caesar himself, after initial trials and appeals failed to reach a satisfactory decision. This was in effect an appeal to the supreme court of the Roman Empire." Dr. David Guzik, *Enduring Word* commentary

Nero was the emperor of Rome from 54–68 A.D. In the early years of his rule, he was considered admirable. Only after 62 A.D. did he turn against Christianity.

A DEEPER LOOK

Paul's accusers were relentless. Even with a change in leadership, their resentment and hostility toward Paul and his Gospel message persisted. It would be one thing if the charges against him were true. But these men—supposed spiritual leaders of the people—leveled false indictments against Paul with a singular goal: destroy the man and his ministry.

As believers, we experience the same kind of harassment from our constant accuser and greatest enemy, Satan. He hates all those who follow Christ, and his chief aim is our personal destruction. He fights incessantly against us with cunning deceit, attempting to blind us to what is true about our lives in Christ.

We aren't defenseless in this war; God has given us powerful weapons in His Word and by His Spirit. Choose at least ONE verse below and answer: What does the Bible teach us about Christ's victory over Satan? How does this reality help us combat his false accusations against us?

Ephesians 6:11–12   1 Peter 5:8–9
Colossians 2:15   1 John 3:8
James 4:7   Revelation 20:10

This line from an old hymn titled *I Hear the Accuser Roar* by Samuel Whitlock Gandy, is a beautiful reminder that, because of Christ, sin and Satan no longer have power over us. We can live every moment of every day forgiven and free.

> *Well may the accuser roar*
> *Of things that I have done;*
> *I know them well, and thousands more;*
> *Jehovah knowest none.*

STUDY THREE | Acts 25:13–26:3
Pomp and Sovereign Circumstances

A speedy trial was not in the cards for Paul. As an innocent man, the apostle had now spent more than two years imprisoned at Caesarea (Acts 24:27) but, in this scene, we catch a glimpse of why. Throughout his ministry, Paul shared the Gospel with hundreds, even thousands, at a time. Sometimes the crowds were welcoming and curious, others were hostile and violent. The bystanders participating in the spectacle here could receive the benefit and blessing of his sermon but, this time, Paul's focus is on one Jewish king with a long connection to the Christ. Lifeless hearts throughout the Roman Empire would take notice if royalty found redemption. What effect would truth have on this one man in this crucial moment?

---

13 Now when several days had elapsed, King Agrippa and Bernice arrived at Caesarea and paid their respects to Festus. **14** While they were spending many days there, Festus laid Paul's case before the king, saying, "There is a man who was left as a prisoner by Felix; **15** and when I was at Jerusalem, the chief priests and the elders of the Jews brought charges against him, asking for a sentence of condemnation against him. **16** I answered them that it is not the custom of the Romans to hand over any man before the accused meets his accusers face to face and has an opportunity to make his defense against the charges. **17** So after they had assembled here, I did not delay, but on the next day took my seat on the tribunal and ordered the man to be brought before me. **18** When the accusers stood up, they began bringing charges against him not of such crimes as I was expecting, **19** but they simply had some points of disagreement with him about their own religion and about a dead man, Jesus, whom Paul asserted to be alive. **20** Being at a loss how to investigate such matters, I asked whether he was willing to go to Jerusalem and there stand trial on these matters. **21** But when Paul appealed to be held in custody for the Emperor's decision, I ordered him to be kept in custody until I send him to Caesar." **22** Then Agrippa said to Festus, "I also would like to hear the man myself." "Tomorrow," he said, "you shall hear him."

23 So, on the next day when Agrippa came together with Bernice amid great pomp, and entered the auditorium accompanied by the commanders and the prominent men of the city, at the command of Festus, Paul was brought in. **24** Festus said, "King Agrippa, and all you gentlemen here present with us, you see this man about whom all the people of the Jews appealed to me, both at Jerusalem and here, loudly declaring that he ought not to live any longer. **25** But I found that he had committed nothing worthy of death; and since he himself appealed to the Emperor, I decided to send him. **26** Yet I have nothing definite about him to write to my lord. Therefore I have brought him before you all and especially before you, King Agrippa, so that after the investigation has taken place, I may have something to write. **27** For it seems absurd to me in sending a prisoner, not to indicate also the charges against him."

26 Agrippa said to Paul, "You are permitted to speak for yourself." Then Paul stretched out his hand and proceeded to make his defense:

2 "In regard to all the things of which I am accused by the Jews, I consider myself fortunate, King Agrippa, that I am about to make my defense before you today; **3** especially because you are an expert in all customs and questions among the Jews; therefore I beg you to listen to me patiently.

---

1. Who arrived in Caesarea and what issue did he and Festus discuss during his visit? (vv. 13–21)

> Agrippa II was the son of Herod Agrippa who killed James the apostle and died after being eaten by worms in Acts 12:23. He was the great grandson of Herod the Great, who was king when Jesus was born. King Agrippa II ruled over primarily Gentile territories and was very loyal to Rome. Agrippa II also ruled over the temple in Jerusalem and was granted the right by Rome to choose the high priest. Agrippa II is the last of the Herods recorded in Scripture. Bernice was his half-sister and constant companion.

2. Read and underline the original charges against Paul by the Jews in Acts 21:28.

   "'...Men of Israel, come to our aid! This is the man who preaches to all men everywhere against our people and the Law and this place; and besides he has even brought Greeks into the temple and has defiled this holy place.'"

3. How did Festus describe Jesus? (v. 19)

4. How do the verses below confirm that Paul was right and Festus was wrong about Jesus in verse 19?

   "He is not here, for He has risen, just as He said. Come, see the place where He was lying." Matthew 28:6

   "Therefore we have been buried with Him through baptism into death, so that as Christ was raised from the dead through the glory of the Father, so we too might walk in newness of life. For if we have become united with Him in the likeness of His death, certainly we shall also be in the likeness of His resurrection..." Romans 6:4–5

   "...and that He was buried, and that He was raised on the third day according to the Scriptures..." 1 Corinthians 15:4

"'...I am the first and the last, and the living One; and I was dead, and behold, I am alive forever-more, and I have the keys of death and of Hades.'" Revelation 1:17–18

> In Greek, the imperfect tense used in this sentence means, "I have been wanting to hear Paul for a long time." His reputation preceded him.

5. How did King Agrippa respond to this report of Festus' prisoner? (v. 22)

6. Who else was in attendance for Paul's audience before Agrippa? (v. 23)

7. How did Festus' conclusion about Paul differ from the Jews' demands? (vv. 24–25)

8. What was the governor's dilemma? (Acts 25:26–27)

9. Because of his audience, Paul was going to present his testimony with a certain emphasis. What did Paul point out about King Agrippa's background in verses 2–3?

STUDY | Acts 26:4–23
FOUR | Paul's Heavenly Vision, Revisited

This is the third time Paul's conversion story is recorded in Acts. The first time is Luke's telling in Acts 9 as it happened chronologically in Scripture. The second is Acts 22 when Paul returned to Jerusalem after his missionary journeys and gave his testimony to a violent Jewish mob. This last account is a more private setting and directed to an audience of one. Each telling is accurate but different in purpose and emphasis. And anyone with an open heart will discover themselves in the details. Those who cling to their own self-righteousness can find conviction in Paul's humility. Those who fear their sin has gone beyond grace can find hope in Paul's rescue. And those who believe they are not worthy of salvation need only listen to the words of life Jesus came to proclaim: *Turn to Me and be saved.*

4 "So then, all Jews know my manner of life from my youth up, which from the beginning was spent among my own nation and at Jerusalem; **5** since they have known about me for a long time, if they are willing to testify, that I lived as a Pharisee according to the strictest sect of our religion. **6** And now I am standing trial for the hope of the promise made by God to our fathers; **7** the promise to which our twelve tribes hope to attain, as they earnestly serve God night and day. And for this hope, O King, I am being accused by Jews. **8** Why is it considered incredible among you people if God does raise the dead?

9 "So then, I thought to myself that I had to do many things hostile to the name of Jesus of Nazareth. **10** And this is just what I did in Jerusalem; not only did I lock up many of the saints in prisons, having received authority from the chief priests, but also when they were being put to death I cast my vote against them. **11** And as I punished them often in all the synagogues, I tried to force them to blaspheme; and being furiously enraged at them, I kept pursuing them even to foreign cities.

12 "While so engaged as I was journeying to Damascus with the authority and commission of the chief priests, **13** at midday, O King, I saw on the way a light from heaven, brighter than the sun, shining all around me and those who were journeying with me. **14** And when we had all fallen to the ground, I heard a voice saying to me in the Hebrew dialect, 'Saul, Saul, why are you persecuting Me? It is hard for you to kick against the goads.' **15** And I said, 'Who are You, Lord?' And the Lord said, 'I am Jesus whom you are persecuting. **16** But get up and stand on your feet; for this purpose I have appeared to you, to appoint you a minister and a witness not only to the things which you have seen, but also to the things in which I will appear to you; **17** rescuing you from the Jewish people and from the Gentiles, to whom I am sending you, **18** to open their eyes so that they may turn from darkness to light and from the dominion of Satan to God, that they may receive forgiveness of sins and an inheritance among those who have been sanctified by faith in Me.'

19 "So, King Agrippa, I did not prove disobedient to the heavenly vision, **20** but kept declaring both to those of Damascus first, and also at Jerusalem and then throughout all the region of Judea, and even to the Gentiles, that they should repent and turn to God, performing deeds appropriate to repentance. **21** For this reason some Jews seized me in the temple and tried to put me to death. **22** So, having obtained help from God, I stand to this day testifying both to small and great, stating nothing but what the Prophets and Moses said was going to take place; **23** that the Christ was to suffer, and that by reason of His resurrection from the dead He would be the first to proclaim light both to the Jewish people and to the Gentiles."

1. Why would the Jews Paul referred to in verses 4–5 be reluctant to testify about Paul's "manner of life from his youth?" What does Paul say he has in common with his Jewish accusers? (v. 5)

2. Circle the word "our" in verses 5–7 and underline what it refers to. How does that inclusive word help his audience understand how Paul still feels about his Jewish heritage?

3. Why does Paul say he is standing trial and what word is repeated three times in those verses? (vv. 6–7)

4. What did Paul—as Saul—formerly consider his duty and who were his accomplices? (vv. 9–12)

5. Paul again described his encounter with Jesus on the road to Damascus in Acts 26:12–15. He introduced an interesting phrase not seen previously that the Lord challenged him with in verse 14. Write that phrase below.

According to Baker's *Exegetical Commentary on the New Testament* by Dr. Darrell Bock, "*A goad is a stick that serves the same purpose as a whip and is used to prod and direct an animal. So in the appearance Jesus was asking why Saul is kicking against God's discipline and direction.*"

In what ways do you "kick against the goads" in your walk with Christ?

6. What promises—direct and indirect—about his life and his ministry did Jesus make to Paul as He commissioned him and how is Paul fulfilling them? (vv. 16–18)

7. What all does the Gospel offer to those who will trust in Christ, according to verse 18?

8. How did Paul say he responded to Jesus' offer and how does this parallel the progression in Acts 1:8? (vv. 19–20))

9. Paul explained the immediate and the eternal reasons he was standing in Caesarea in chains in Acts 26:20–23. What are those reasons?

   Immediate (v. 20):

   Eternal (vv. 22–23):

10. How does Paul describe the inclusiveness of the Gospel in Acts 26:23?

STUDY FIVE | Acts 26:24–32
Unpersuaded

You would be hard pressed to find a picture of grace as profound as this. A ruler from the line of Herod was present at every crucial moment in the history of salvation, from the birth of the Messiah in Bethlehem to His murder on a cross outside Jerusalem. And here again stands a Herod—Agrippa II, the last of his kin ever mentioned in Scripture—before God's faithful Gospel minister, who prayed this Herod would at last recognize the truth. Somewhat convinced or almost won over is hardly certain and secure. How tragic that this king with a line straight to the holiest throne would deny all that he had heard and known and turn and walk away.

---

24 While Paul was saying this in his defense, Festus said in a loud voice, "Paul, you are out of your mind! Your great learning is driving you mad." **25** But Paul said, "I am not out of my mind, most excellent Festus, but I utter words of sober truth. **26** For the king knows about these matters, and I speak to him also with confidence, since I am persuaded that none of these things escape his notice; for this has not been done in a corner. **27** King Agrippa, do you believe the Prophets? I know that you do." **28** Agrippa replied to Paul, "In a short time you will persuade me to become a Christian." **29** And Paul said, "I would wish

Empowered: The Amazing Church of Jesus Christ

to God, that whether in a short or long time, not only you, but also all who hear me this day, might become such as I am, except for these chains."

30 The king stood up and the governor and Bernice, and those who were sitting with them, **31** and when they had gone aside, they began talking to one another, saying, "This man is not doing anything worthy of death or imprisonment." **32** And Agrippa said to Festus, "This man might have been set free if he had not appealed to Caesar."

---

1. What conclusion did Festus come to after Paul presented his testimony? (v. 24) Read 1 Corinthians 1:18 below for further understanding as to why someone like Festus would think this way.

   "For the word of the cross is foolishness to those who are perishing, but to us who are being saved it is the power of God."

2. Paul turned his attention to King Agrippa in verses 26–27 and appealed to his prior knowledge about his religious understanding and actual events that occurred in his lifetime. Paul asked a pointed question of King Agrippa in verse 27. Describe the predicament the king's answer would have put him in.

3. Verse 28 is a significant moment. And Agrippa appears to understand what Paul is trying to do. How does the king respond to Paul and what does it reveal about his heart?

4. Verse 29 reveals the true intent of Paul's heart from the very beginning. What was Paul's prayer and hope for everyone in the room?

5. What conclusion did the assembly appear to collectively come to in Acts 26:30–31?

6. What did they avoid discussing?

7. Who did Agrippa blame in verse 32 for Paul's remaining in custody?

8. There were several responses to the resurrection in this storyline.

   How did the Jewish religious leaders respond? (Acts 24:5–9)

   How did the political leaders, Festus and Agrippa, respond? (Acts 26:24, 28)

   What are some of the ways the world responds to the resurrection?

A DEEPER LOOK

Using Romans 12:9–14, consider how Paul models the Christian life for us. Circle all of the action words that you see below:

"Let love be without hypocrisy. Abhor what is evil; cling to what is good. Be devoted to one another in brotherly love; give preference to one another in honor; not lagging behind in diligence, fervent in spirit, serving the Lord; rejoicing in hope, persevering in tribulation, devoted to prayer, contributing to the needs of the saints, practicing hospitality. Bless those who persecute you; bless and do not curse."

How does Paul display these qualities in his trial with King Agrippa that we studied this week?

Think about the challenges in your life right now. Are there any of these "actions" you could take? Pray through Romans 12:9–14 and ask the Lord to give you His wisdom, direction, and attitude for your circumstances.

WEEK 12 TEACHING NOTES

Map of Paul's Journey to Rome

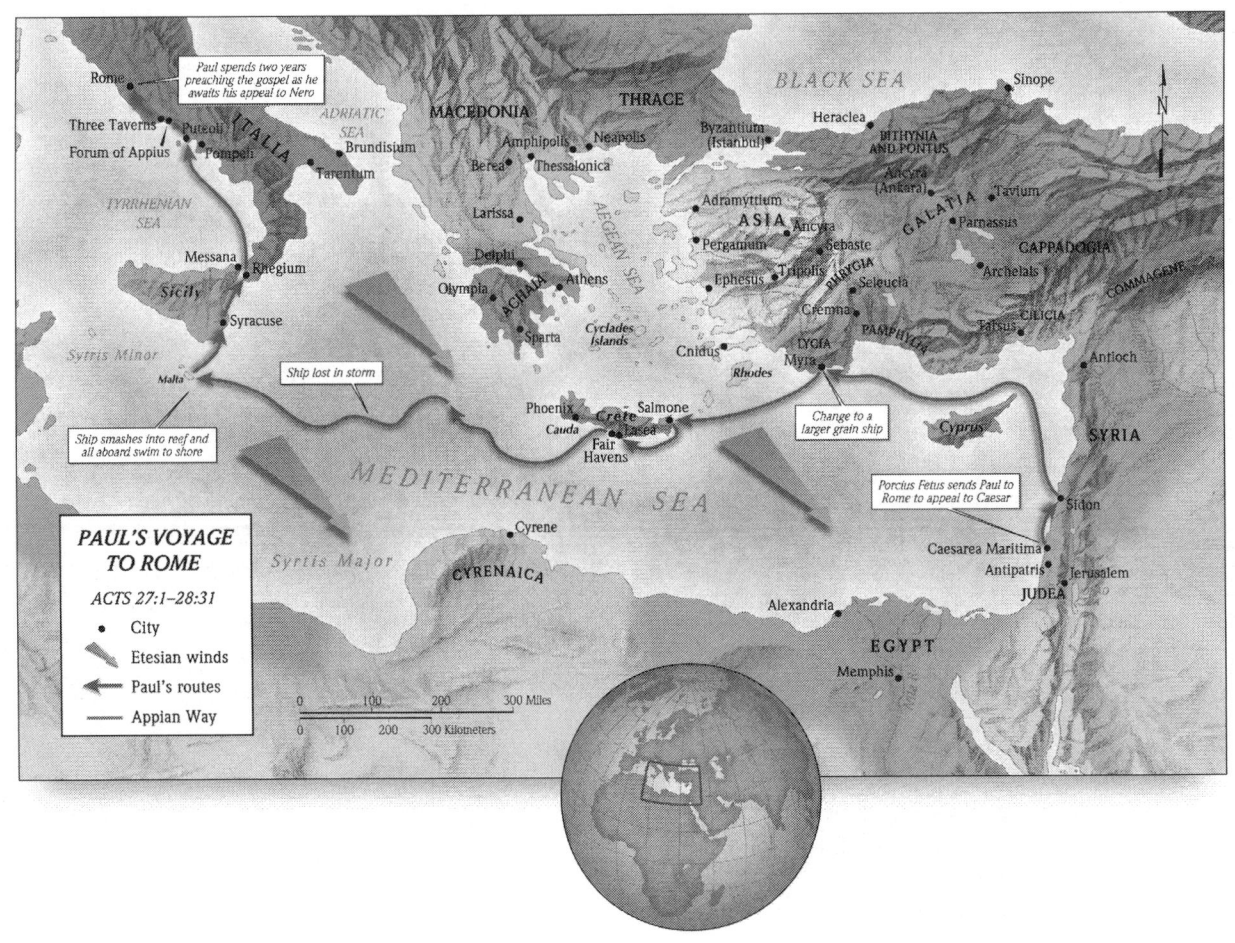

Empowered: The Amazing Church of Jesus Christ

Acts 27–28

Paul's Journey to Rome

The end of Acts contains one of the most detailed accounts of a shipwreck in ancient history. A passenger himself, Luke meticulously recorded every blast of wind and roiling wave that Paul and the other 275 souls on board endured for weeks on end. As the ship lurched wildly through the sea, the only thing Paul had to cling to was God's promise that He would safely deliver him to Rome.

And he did arrive at last, still in chains, but sharing the unfettered Gospel message with the Roman Jews and then any and all who found their way to his doorstep. As he writes in Philippians, "...my circumstances have turned out for the greater progress of the gospel... ." Rather than extinguishing the message, Paul's captivity shone a spotlight on the glory of Christ, bringing even palace guards and fellow prisoners out of darkness. (Philippians 1:12–14)

KEY VERSE:

"And he stayed two full years...and was welcoming all who came to him, preaching the kingdom of God and teaching concerning the Lord Jesus Christ with all openness, unhindered."

ACTS 28:30–31

STUDY ONE | Acts 27:1–12
Bound for Rome

Paul was on the move again at last. His extended stay in Caesarea might have seemed to some like an obstacle or unnecessary, but it was God's hand that held him there. He had provided Paul with divine assurance he would reach Rome (Acts 23:11), so there was surely divine intent behind that "detour." Now, the Lord's timing meant His servant would sail across the Mediterranean on the cusp of a treacherous time of year for sea travel. God graciously placed a benevolent guardian over Paul during his voyage who allowed him to receive mercy and also dispense wisdom. Even in chains, Paul was a leader—not by his own power, but by the Spirit working in him: God's strength once again on display in Paul's weakness.

1 When it was decided that we would sail for Italy, they proceeded to deliver Paul and some other prisoners to a centurion of the Augustan cohort named Julius. **2** And embarking in an Adramyttian ship, which was about to sail to the regions along the coast of Asia, we put out to sea accompanied by Aristarchus, a Macedonian of Thessalonica. **3** The next day we put in at Sidon; and Julius treated Paul with consideration and allowed him to go to his friends and receive care. **4** From there we put out to sea and sailed under the shelter of Cyprus because the winds were contrary. **5** When we had sailed through the sea along the coast of Cilicia and Pamphylia, we landed at Myra in Lycia. **6** There the centurion found an Alexandrian ship sailing for Italy, and he put us aboard it. **7** When we had sailed slowly for a good many days, and with difficulty had arrived off Cnidus, since the wind did not permit us to go farther, we sailed under the shelter of Crete, off Salmone; **8** and with difficulty sailing past it we came to a place called Fair Havens, near which was the city of Lasea.

9 When considerable time had passed and the voyage was now dangerous, since even the fast was already over, Paul began to admonish them, **10** and said to them, "Men, I perceive that the voyage will certainly be with damage and great loss, not only of the cargo and the ship, but also of our lives." **11** But the centurion was more persuaded by the pilot and the captain of the ship than by what was being said by Paul. **12** Because the harbor was not suitable for wintering, the majority reached a decision to put out to sea from there, if somehow they could reach Phoenix, a harbor of Crete, facing southwest and northwest, and spend the winter there.

1. After spending two years in prison in Caesarea (Acts 24:27), Paul exercised his right as a Roman citizen to make an appeal before Caesar (see Acts 25:6–12 for review) and was finally headed to Rome, Italy.

   Who was going with him? (Acts 27:1–2)

2. Look up the following verses and note where we have seen Aristarchus in Scripture. What do you learn about his connection to Paul and the Gospel ministry?

   Acts 19:28–29

   Acts 20:3–4

Colossians 4:10

Philemon 1:23–24

3. What do you learn about Paul, Julius, and the believers in Sidon? (Acts 27:3)

Verses 4–5 describe the route along the southern coast of modern-day Turkey. Sailing the ship "under the shelter of Cyprus" refers to the practice of sailing near the island so that it provides protection from the winds. The Alexandrian ship Paul was put aboard in Myra in verse 6 was from northern Egypt, which was the largest provider of grain for Rome. Historians estimate these ships displaced up to 600 tons. The *Mayflower*, by contrast, displaced 250 tons.

4. What was the journey like after leaving Myra and why, according to verses 7–8?

Sea travel was perilous in the ancient world in a way we can never fully appreciate. Travel in the Mediterranean was not typically attempted after mid-September. Voyages were completely avoided from mid-November until mid-March. Scholars estimate Paul's journey took place around mid-October.

5. The reference to the "fast" in verse 9 points to the Day of Atonement, which falls in late September—early October. Travel conditions had deteriorated considerably during their time in Fair Havens, according to verse 9. How were conditions described?

The word "admonish" used here means to emphasize something again and again with strong emotion and earnestness. By this time, Paul had survived three shipwrecks (2 Corinthians 11:25), so his seafaring experience and intuition was worth noting.

6. What was Paul's response to the situation and why? (vv. 9b–10)

7. How did the crew and ship's officers respond to Paul? (Acts 27:11–12)

8. Paul's warning and advice went unheeded, but it appears he still had a seat at the decision-making table. Why would Paul have enjoyed this level of privilege?

9. Paul had been assured he would eventually make it to Rome but, here, he acted with the benefit of everyone on board in mind. As His children, what expectation does God have of us when we see a need, regardless of our circumstances?

10. What was the plan for winter? (v. 12)

> Fair Havens was fifty miles away from Phoenix. The trip usually took a day or half a day.

STUDY TWO | Acts 27:13–26
Dangers, Toils, and Snares

Those with sensitive constitutions should take heed before reading this passage. With harrowing detail, Luke recorded what happens when a 180-foot wooden ship crosses paths with the force of a hurricane. Its violent, icy winds turned the sea into a cyclone strong enough to break their sailing vessel—and the courage of those on board—into pieces. Days on end without light, rest, or food led to weary bodies and hopeless hearts. Until, in their darkest moment, the Lord sent Paul a lifeline. As the ship hurled through the relentless waves, Paul shared the promise of peace he received from the only One who could—and would—deliver them all.

---

13 When a moderate south wind came up, supposing that they had attained their purpose, they weighed anchor and began sailing along Crete, close inshore.

14 But before very long there rushed down from the land a violent wind, called Euraquilo; **15** and when the ship was caught in it and could not face the wind, we gave way to it and let ourselves be driven along. **16** Running under the shelter of a small island called Clauda, we were scarcely able to get the ship's boat under control. **17** After they had hoisted it up, they used supporting cables in undergirding the ship; and fearing that they might run aground on the shallows of Syrtis, they let down the sea anchor and in this way let themselves be driven along. **18** The next day as we were being violently storm-tossed, they began to jettison the cargo; **19** and on the third day they threw the ship's tackle overboard with their own hands. **20** Since neither sun nor stars appeared for many days, and no small storm was assailing us, from then on all hope of our being saved was gradually abandoned.

21 When they had gone a long time without food, then Paul stood up in their midst and said, "Men, you ought to have followed my advice and not to have set sail from Crete and incurred this damage and loss. **22** Yet now I urge you to keep up your courage, for there will be no loss of life among you, but only of the ship. **23** For this very night an angel of the God to whom I belong and whom I serve stood before me, **24** saying, 'Do not be afraid, Paul; you must stand before Caesar; and behold, God has granted you all those who are sailing with you.' **25** Therefore, keep up your courage, men, for I believe God that it will turn out exactly as I have been told. **26** But we must run aground on a certain island."

1. The weather conditions of verse 13 seemed to confirm their decision to sail to Phoenix. But we soon learn that only an illusion of calm weather had lured them away from safe harbor. What caught everyone by surprise in verses 14–15?

2. Read verses 16–20 out loud. Imagine being a passenger on this ship. How would you describe your experience in detail?

> "It is probably as they round the cape that they meet a wind of hurricane force, called the 'Northeaster,' blowing down from 8,056-foot Mount Ida. The strong cold wind that blows across the Mediterranean in the winter from a general northeasterly direction is caused by a depression ("low") over Libya which induces a strong flow of air from Greece."
> William J. Larkin, *IVP New Testament Commentary Series – Acts*

3. How did the crew spend the next forty-eight hours? (vv. 18–19)

> The tackle of a ship has multiple interpretations, but here, most biblical historians agree this referred to ropes, cables, and any other spare gear as well as furniture like beds, tables, and chairs. In other words, they threw overboard whatever would weigh them down that they could do without.

4. How were the conditions described in verses 20–21?

5. How did Paul emphasize his credibility here with the crew?

6. How did Paul inspire and encourage the crew in verses 22–27?

7. The Lord gave these pagan sailors a concrete reminder of His presence and power through Paul. Verse 24 tells us that Paul's presence on the ship—and prayers for his fellow passengers—provided the blessing of preservation for everyone on board.

Jeremiah 29:7 offers an example of practical direction for graciously living in the world — "Seek the welfare of the city where I have sent you into exile, and pray to the Lord on its behalf; for in its welfare you will have welfare."

In what ways should the presence of believers provide blessing to the people and circumstances we encounter?

8. Since his conversion in Acts 9, Paul has endured many storms and trials, but has remained steadfast and faithful. How have his responses encouraged you to remain faithful in your storms of life?

STUDY THREE | Acts 27:27–44
Shipwreck

Wide awake at midnight—with no light or instruments to guide them—the sailors' experienced ears alerted them to a harsh reality: their out-of-control vessel was quickly approaching land. Hope faded against the prospect of imminent destruction, but a reminder of God's promise righted their reasoning. Paul took the time to pause, pray, and praise the Lord with 275 of his fellow sojourners, which nourished their bodies and souls. The crew did all they could to avoid collision, but the ship fell victim to the elements and the sea. And whether they swam, floated, or hung on for dear life, the Lord carried every man safely to the shore, as promised.

---

27 But when the fourteenth night came, as we were being driven about in the Adriatic Sea, about midnight the sailors began to surmise that they were approaching some land. 28 They took soundings and found it to be twenty fathoms; and a little farther on they took another sounding and found it to be fifteen fathoms. 29 Fearing that we might run aground somewhere on the rocks, they cast four anchors from the stern and wished for daybreak. 30 But as the sailors were trying to escape from the ship and had let down the ship's boat into the sea, on the pretense of intending to lay out anchors from the bow, 31 Paul said to the centurion and to the soldiers, "Unless these men remain in the ship, you yourselves cannot be saved." 32 Then the soldiers cut away the ropes of the ship's boat and let it fall away.

33 Until the day was about to dawn, Paul was encouraging them all to take some food, saying, "Today is the fourteenth day that you have been constantly watching and going without eating, having taken nothing. 34 Therefore I encourage you to take some food, for this is for your preservation, for not a hair from the head of any of you will perish." 35 Having said this, he took bread and gave thanks to God in the presence of all, and he broke it and began to eat. 36 All of them were encouraged and they themselves also took food. 37 All of us in the ship were two hundred and seventy-six persons. 38 When they had eaten enough, they began to lighten the ship by throwing out the wheat into the sea.

Empowered: The Amazing Church of Jesus Christ

39 When day came, they could not recognize the land; but they did observe a bay with a beach, and they resolved to drive the ship onto it if they could. **40** And casting off the anchors, they left them in the sea while at the same time they were loosening the ropes of the rudders; and hoisting the foresail to the wind, they were heading for the beach. **41** But striking a reef where two seas met, they ran the vessel aground; and the prow stuck fast and remained immovable, but the stern began to be broken up by the force of the waves. **42** The soldiers' plan was to kill the prisoners, so that none of them would swim away and escape; **43** but the centurion, wanting to bring Paul safely through, kept them from their intention, and commanded that those who could swim should jump overboard first and get to land, **44** and the rest should follow, some on planks, and others on various things from the ship. And so it happened that they all were brought safely to land.

---

1. After fourteen days in a violent storm, what hope/warning did those on board "hear" in the middle of the night? (vv. 27–28)

> Fathom and sounding are nautical terms related to measuring the depth of the water. A fathom is a measurement of about six feet. Sailors took soundings by dropping a line overboard with a lead weight attached. In Greek, "took soundings" literally means "hearing the land."

2. Verse 29 tells us the ship and her crew were still in harm's way. How did the panicked sailors respond to these circumstances in verse 30 despite Paul's previous assurance in verses 22–26?

3. What condition of the Lord's promise did Paul declare and how do we know those on the ship finally took Paul's words to heart? (vv.31–32)

4. As the sea continued to rage around them, Paul once again stepped into a pastoral role in verse 33. What did he counsel the sailors to do and why? (vv. 33–34)

5. In verses 35–36 Paul has an opportunity to point the passengers to Jesus. In extraordinary circumstances, Paul reminded his fellow prisoners and passengers to give thanks in all things. Why would this be such an encouragement to those on board?

6. Full bellies, cheered hearts, and the light of day gave the crew a new confidence in verse 39. What course of action did they determine next?

 7. In your own words, summarize what happened in verses 40–41. Use the definitions provided to help clarify the events.

Anchor: Unlike today's ships, ancient sailing vessels had numerous anchors. They were often made of stone and were lighter than modern iron anchors. They were used to slow down or ground a ship.

Rudders: A rudder functions as the steering wheel of the ship and is used to direct its course. In this case, rudders refer to paddle rudders or oversized oars that were attached to the right and left sides of the ship. The ropes kept them in place and allowed them to move.

Foresail: A foresail is attached to the bow or front of the ship. Smaller than the main sail, it's used for guidance and speed.

Reef: Other translations use the term "sand bar." Scholars also note the phrase in verse 41—"where the two seas meet"—could refer to cross currents. Some combination of mucky bay floor and direction of the wind and sea created this nautical hazard.

Prow: The front or forward-most part of the ship that cuts through the water.

Stern: The back portion of the vessel.

8. Man's plan and God's plan are at odds once more in verse 42. What did the soldiers want to do as a result of the shipwreck and why?

> Under Roman law, the soldiers were personally responsible for the prisoners; if any escaped, they would pay with their own lives. In their minds, it would be easier to account for a dead prisoner than a missing one.

9. How did the Lord use the Roman centurion to intervene in verses 43–44a? What was the result in verse 44b?

10. Self-preservation is a common human reaction to difficult circumstances with uncertain out-comes. Have you ever tried to save yourself from a difficult situation by not waiting on the Lord to work as He promised? What was the result? What did you learn about yourself? What did you learn about God?

STUDY FOUR | Acts 28:1–16
Thoroughly Safe at Malta

After leaving Clauda and careening off course for two weeks, Paul and the others had travelled about 475 miles when they landed at last at Malta. In the middle of a strong storm, God's sovereign hand mirac-ulously moved this ship from one speck in the sea to another, arriving with every soul safe and sound. God's mercy continued through the hospitality of the natives, who gave and received grace upon grace during their stay. Gospel proclamations are not mentioned but, true to his own exhortation to "be ready in season and out of season" (2 Timothy 4:2), Paul surely spent his days there with eternity in mind. After recovering through the winter, the crew left Malta on another Alexandrian ship in February of 60 A.D., with just 210 miles left to travel before arriving in Rome.

---

1 When they had been brought safely through, then we found out that the island was called Malta. **2** The natives showed us extraordinary kindness; for because of the rain that had set in and because of the cold, they kindled a fire and received us all. **3** But when Paul had gathered a bundle of sticks and laid them on the fire, a viper came out because of the heat and fastened itself on his hand. **4** When the natives saw the creature hanging from his hand, they began saying to one another, "Undoubtedly this man is a murderer, and though he has been saved from the sea, justice has not allowed him to live." **5** However he shook the creature off into the fire and suffered no harm. **6** But they were expecting that he was about to swell up or suddenly fall down dead. But after they had waited a long time and had seen nothing unusual happen to him, they changed their minds and began to say that he was a god.

7 Now in the neighborhood of that place were lands belonging to the lead-ing man of the island, named Publius, who welcomed us and entertained us courteously three days. **8** And it happened that the father of Publius was lying in bed afflicted with recurrent fever and dysentery; and Paul went in to see him and after he had prayed, he laid his hands on him and healed him. **9** After this had happened, the rest of the people on the island who had diseases were coming to him and getting cured. **10** They also honored us with many marks of respect; and when we were setting sail, they supplied us with all we needed.

11 At the end of three months we set sail on an Alexandrian ship which had wintered at the island, and which had the Twin Brothers for its figurehead. **12** After we put in at Syracuse, we stayed there for three days. **13** From there we sailed around and arrived at Rhegium, and a day later a south wind sprang up, and on the second day we came to Puteoli. **14** There we found some brethren, and were invited to stay with them for seven days; and thus we came to Rome. **15** And the brethren, when they heard about us, came from there as far as the Market of Appius and Three Inns to meet us; and when Paul saw them, he thanked God and took courage. **16** When we entered Rome, Paul was allowed to stay by himself, with the soldier who was guarding him.

1. Where did the ship safely land and what is revealed about the citizenry? (vv. 1–2)

> The wording here means the crew were "saved all the way through" or completely delivered. The language used is known as the "divine passive." This means their safe passage had nothing at all to do with their own skills, but was due entirely to the sovereign power of God.

2. When was the last time you were shown extraordinarily kindness? How did you respond?

3. Paul, likely soaked to the bone, gathered sticks for the fire alongside his new friends at Malta. After surviving months as a prisoner in a storm-tossed sea, what happened to Paul and how did the people characterize it? (vv. 3–4)

> Malta is fifty-eight miles south of Sicily and 180 miles northeast of Africa. The island is eighteen miles long and eight miles wide. The name means "refuge."

4. Why did the natives reverse their thinking about Paul—from calling him a murderer to deciding he was a god? (vv. 5–6)

5. Who did the shipwrecked crew meet in verse 7 and how was he described?

6. How did the Lord use His sovereign placement of Paul at Malta to provide for him and others? (vv. 8–9)

7. Verse 2 said the natives greeted the shipwrecked crew with kindness. How did they continue to treat these foreigners and send them off in verse 10?

8. After spending the winter at Malta, Paul and the crew boarded another Alexandrian ship for the final 210 miles of their trip. Use the map on page 196 to chart verses 12–13, the last leg of Paul's journey to Rome. How did God once again encourage Paul in verses 14–15?

> The "Twin Brothers" mentioned here are Castor and Pollux, twin half-brothers in Greek and Roman mythology and also the constellation of Gemini. They were considered by pagans to be "guardian deities," specifically the patron protectors of sailors and their ships.

9. What were Paul's living conditions like in Rome? (Acts 28:16)

> Paul's journey from Caesarea to Rome took more than four months. Scholars estimate the distance as somewhere between 2,130–2,250 miles.

10. All roads may lead to Rome, but these sixty verses of Acts 27 and 28 demonstrate an even more certain reality: God can and does use all circumstances—every detail of our lives—to draw us along in faith to Him. And we can trust His plan even when it might seem like no one is steering the ship.

What happened to your faith as a result of enduring seasons you wouldn't choose but wouldn't change?

STUDY | **Acts 28:17–31**
FIVE | **Openness, Unhindered**

Instead of travelling to parts unknown to share the Gospel, the mission field came to Paul while he was in Rome. The Jews first, as always, with some embracing the hope Paul offered while others followed in the rejection of their fathers. Paul was a prolific writer while under house arrest, penning Ephesians, Philippians, Colossians, and Philemon—sacred texts we read as eagerly today as did the churches from centuries past. God's imprisoned servant enjoyed unrestrained freedom to continue his ministry, boldly teaching about Jesus to everyone whose ears and hearts were open. And the message of grace and hope continues to the uttermost parts of the earth. Paul faithfully ran and finished the race, and we are called to do the same. Because every life depends on it.

17 After three days Paul called together those who were the leading men of the Jews, and when they came together, he began saying to them, "Brethren, though I had done nothing against our people or the customs of our fathers, yet I was delivered as a prisoner from Jerusalem into the hands of the Romans. **18** And when they had examined me, they were willing to release me because there was no ground for putting me to death. **19** But when the Jews objected, I was forced to appeal to Caesar, not that I had any accusation against my nation. **20** For this reason, therefore, I requested to see you and to speak with you, for I am wearing this chain for the sake of the hope of Israel." **21** They said to him, "We have neither received letters from Judea concerning you, nor have any of the brethren come here and reported or spoken anything bad about you. **22** But we desire to hear from you what your views are; for concerning this sect, it is known to us that it is spoken against everywhere."

23 When they had set a day for Paul, they came to him at his lodging in large numbers; and he was explaining to them by solemnly testifying about the kingdom of God and trying to persuade them concerning Jesus, from both the Law of Moses and from the Prophets, from morning until evening. **24** Some were being persuaded by the things spoken, but others would not believe. **25** And when they did not agree with one another, they began leaving after Paul had spoken one parting word, "The Holy Spirit rightly spoke through Isaiah the prophet to your fathers, **26** saying,

'Go to this people and say,
"You will keep on hearing, but will not understand;
And you will keep on seeing, but will not perceive;
27 For the heart of this people has become dull,
And with their ears they scarcely hear,
And they have closed their eyes;
Otherwise they might see with their eyes,
And hear with their ears,
And understand with their heart and return,
And I would heal them."'

28 Therefore let it be known to you that this salvation of God has been sent to the Gentiles; they will also listen." **29** [When he had spoken these words, the Jews departed, having a great dispute among themselves.]

30 And he stayed two full years in his own rented quarters and was welcoming all who came to him, **31** preaching the kingdom of God and teaching concerning the Lord Jesus Christ with all openness, unhindered.

---

1. What had been and continued to be Paul's priority when sharing the Gospel throughout his ministry?

   "When they reached Salamis, they began to proclaim the word of God in the synagogues of the Jews; and they also had John as their helper." Acts 13:5

   "In Iconium they entered the synagogue of the Jews together, and spoke in such a manner that a large number of people believed, both of Jews and of Greeks." Acts 14:1

"And according to Paul's custom, he went to them, and for three Sabbaths reasoned with them from the Scriptures..." Acts 17:2

"And he was reasoning in the synagogue every Sabbath and trying to persuade Jews and Greeks." Acts 18:4

"And he entered the synagogue and continued speaking out boldly for three months, reasoning and persuading them about the kingdom of God." Acts 19:8

2. Why did Paul pursue this strategy, according to Romans 1:16 and Romans 9:3–5?

> "Is there any example of undefeatable hope or unconquerable love like this act of Paul when, in Rome too, he preached first to the Jews?" William Barclay

3. Paul outlined the events that led him to Rome in Acts 28:17b–19. Read the passage then decide whether the statements below are true or false:

   a. Paul had broken the Law: T or F

   b. The Romans found no cause for his execution and were willing to release Paul:
      T or F

   c. The Jews agreed that Paul was innocent: T or F

   d. Paul was forced to appeal to Caesar because the Jews continued to seek to kill him: T or F

   e. Paul was angry at the Jews and appealed to Caesar so that he could press charges against them in revenge: T or F

4. Paul gives the true reason behind his presence there in verse 20. What was it?

5. What did the Jewish leaders reveal in Acts 28:21–22 that probably made them more open to hear from Paul?

Answer Key—a: F; b: T; c: F; d: T; e: F.

6. How did Paul present the Gospel to the large number of Jews who came to see him? (v. 23)

   "He was _____ to them by _____ _____ about the kingdom of God and _____ _____ _____ them concerning Jesus."

7. How did the Roman Jews respond to Paul's message in verses 24–25?

By some counts, there are more than 300 Old Testament prophecies about the birth, life, and death of Jesus Christ.

8. There is a pattern in Israel's history recorded in Isaiah, and Paul quoted it to the Jews as his "parting word" in verses 25b–28. What might Paul have hoped to accomplish by holding up the "mirror" of Isaiah 6:9–10 to the Jews in Rome?

The majority of conservative biblical scholars do not believe verse 29 is in the original text of Acts. Many translations either place it in brackets or leave it out of the passage completely.

9. The content of Paul's speech once again stirs up controversy. What did Paul want these Jews to know about the trajectory of the Gospel? (Acts 28:28)

10. The Lord gave Paul two years in Rome and provided the means for him to live on his own. How does verse 31 describe Paul, still a prisoner, and his ability to spread the Gospel?

The book of Acts ends twenty-nine years after the death and resurrection of Jesus and the coming of the Holy Spirit at Pentecost.

A DEEPER LOOK

Imagine the Bible without Acts. If the New Testament moved from the Gospels, ending with John, to Romans and onward, what pieces would be missing? What questions would you have?

How does the book of Acts strengthen your faith in and your love for Jesus and His Church?

Empowered: The Amazing Church of Jesus Christ

As members of the body of the Christ, we are charged to carry out the mission of Christ not only in the world, but among and between one another as believers as well. Choose at least ONE of the verses below and record what it teaches about our role as followers of Jesus in the ongoing mission of the Church.

Romans 12:13

1 Timothy 5:17

Romans 16:17

Hebrews 10:23–25

Galatians 6:1

1 Peter 4:10–11

THE GOSPEL AFTER ACTS: WHAT HAPPENED NEXT?

When Acts ends, Paul is still alive. His prison letters state he was anticipating release—"At the same time also prepare me a lodging, for I hope that through your prayers I will be given to you" (Philemon 1:22)—and he was indeed set free after two years (60–62 A.D.). Paul continued to minister for several more years after that. And though there is no biblical record of it, some scholars believe he travelled to Spain to proclaim the Gospel, as Romans 15:24 says he hoped to do.

In July of 64 A.D., a massive fire destroyed Rome. According to tradition—possibly in an attempt to deflect criticism and responsibility from himself—Nero turned against the Christians and blamed them for the devastation.

In The Annals of Tacitus 15.44, written in approximately 116 A.D., the Roman historian records how this event impacted the Christian population:

> *"But all human efforts, all the lavish gifts of the emperor, and the propitiations of the gods, did not banish the sinister belief that the conflagration (the fire) was the result of an order (given by Nero). Consequently, to get rid of the report, Nero fastened the guilt and inflicted the most exquisite tortures on a class hated for their abominations, called Christians by the populace ... Accordingly, an arrest was first made of all who pleaded guilty (of faith in Jesus); then, upon their information, an immense multitude was convicted, not so much for the crime of firing the city, as of hatred against mankind. Mockery of every sort was added to their deaths. Covered with the skins of beasts, they were torn by dogs and perished, or were nailed to crosses, or were doomed to the flames and burnt, to serve as a nightly illumination, when daylight had expired." Tacitus, Cornelius. The Annals Of Tacitus, Book XIV.*

Some believe Paul's death was related to this specific persecution, that the apostle was rounded up and rearrested with the other believers and killed for his teaching and faith. The true reason for his second confinement at the hand of Rome remains unclear. What is certain is Paul's state of mind and heart.

Unlike his expectations during his first Roman imprisonment, Paul seems to know and accept his fate, as seen in his words in 2 Timothy—the last letter he ever wrote:

> "For I am already being poured out as a drink offering, and the time of my departure has come. I have fought the good fight, I have finished the course, I have kept the faith; in the future there is laid up for me the crown of righteousness, which the Lord, the righteous Judge, will award to me on that day; and not only to me, but also to all who have loved His appearing." 2 Timothy 4:6–8

The Bible does not tell us the exact time or manner of his death, but the commonly held belief comes from the works of Eusebius, an early church historian. He wrote that Paul was beheaded by the order of Nero sometime in May or June of 68 A.D. And we can trust that Paul, with unwavering faith, testified to the grace and truth of the Gospel of Jesus Christ with his very last breath.

Some say the end of Acts feels unfinished. That's because it is. Since the day the Lord opened his eyes, Paul's mission was to take the Gospel to friends and enemies, to those nearby and those at the end of the known world. Now it's our turn.

WHERE DO WE GO FROM HERE?

We get to finish this story.

Until Christ returns, we are called to carry hope and life everywhere we go—from the clerk in our neighborhood grocery store to bustling city streets and remote mountain villages halfway around the world. And as we go with the Gospel, His Spirit goes with us—guiding our steps and giving us His words, just as He was faithful to do for Peter, Barnabas, and Paul, for Philip, Priscilla, and Aquila, and countless unnamed saints thousands of years ago.

May we be as faithful as our brothers and sisters—who counted loss as gain, suffering as joy, and death as life!

The Events of Acts

Week	Section
01	**Acts 1:1 – 2:47 Preparing to Witness & Pentecost**

- Recap Gospels
- Jesus' Final Words & Ascension
- Pentecost
- Peter's 1st Sermon (fulfilment of Scriptures)

02	**Acts 3:1 – 5:42 Jerusalem Ministry**

- Peter & John praying and arrested in the temple
- Healing of the lame man
- Jesus the cornerstone rejected
- The fake piousness of Ananias and Sapphira
- The apostles arrested and released from prison by angel of the Lord

03	**Acts 6:1 – 8:3 Stephen's Ministry**

- Believers growing in numbers
- Distribution of food – social injustice addressed by church
- Choosing of the deacons
- Stephen stoned to death

04	**Acts 8:4 – 9:31 Three unlikely converts: Samaritans, an Ethiopian, and Saul**

- Philip's Ministry to the Samaritans
- Importance of apostolic authority when God approved the Samaritans by giving the Spirit
- Philip meets the eunuch reading Isaiah
- Paul meets Jesus on the road to Damascus

05	**Acts 9:32 – 12:25 Peter's Ministry**

- Peter travels to preach the word and heal the sick
- Peter's vision about sharing with Gentiles
- Barnabas went to Tarsus to find Saul and bring him to Antioch
- Barnabas and Saul take gift to Jerusalem
- James (brother of John) put to death
- Peter arrested and broken out by angel of the Lord.

06	**Acts 13:1 – 14:28 Paul and Barnabas First Missionary Journey**

- Antioch becomes a missionary sending church
- Visits Cyprus and Saul's name is changed to Paul
- After visiting the newly converted cities, Paul return to Antioch to rest
- Very quick paced trip, traveling about 15 miles per day without extended stays. Total of 895 miles traveled.

07   Acts 15: 1-35 Jerusalem Council
- Debate over accepting Gentiles
- Judean men teaching the necessity of circumcision
- Peter's Witness
- James, brother of Jesus – head of the Jerusalem church proclaims a ruling
- Decision given to Antioch

08   Acts 15:36-18:22 Paul's Second Missionary Journey (The Greek World)
- Paul and Barnabas divided over John Mark
- Paul revisits Derbe, Lystra, and Iconium, then called to Macedonia
- Paul meets Lydia
- Paul and Silas beaten and arrested, but still praise God and jailer is converted
- Paul visits Thessalonica, Berea, and Athens
- Paul visits Corinth and meets Priscilla and Aquila
- Paul returns to Antioch

09   Acts 18:23 – 21:16 Paul's Third Missionary Journey
- Paul goes to Ephesus
- Craftsman incite a riot over Paul's teaching
- Paul returns to Macedonia and Achaia
- Trip to Miletus
- Farewell address to Ephesian elders
- Voyage to Jerusalem

10   Acts 21:17 – 23:35 Paul's Arrest in Jerusalem
- Concern of Jerusalem elders
- Temple Riot
- Paul addresses the crowd and the council
- Conspiracy to kill Paul
- Paul sent to Caesarea

11   Acts 24:1 – 26:32 Paul in Caesarea
- Trial in Caesarea before Felix and then Festus
- Paul appeals to Caesar
- Paul appears before Festus and King Agrippa
- Paul declared innocent – but the appeal to Caesar stands

12   Acts 27:1 – 28:31 Paul in Rome
- Paul's journey to Rome
- Shipwreck
- Safe landing at Malta and received great hospitality
- Final leg of journey to Rome
- Paul meets with brothers and with Jews in Rome
- Paul witnesses for 2 years with openness

BIG DREAM
MINISTRIES

Big Dream Ministries exists to help people understand the Bible as God's complete and amazing story of redemption through Jesus Christ and equip them to apply Biblical truths to their lives. We do this by offering studies that drive people to the Scriptures for answers and providing reviews to reinforce the learning. Our vision is for people to be AMAZED

Find Bible Studies and more at **BigDreamMinistries.org**

OUR COLLECTION OF BIBLE STUDIES

THE AMAZING COLLECTION, THE BIBLE, BOOK BY BOOK

Composed of 11 separate studies each teaching a section of the Bible. Together, The Amazing Collection covers every book of the Bible.

Also available in Spanish (La Coleccion Maravillosa: La Biblia, Libro pro Libro)

THE AMAZING ADVENTURE

An early childhood (3 – 7 years) curriculum with lessons, activities, and music to teach every book of the Bible.

BE AMAZING

Based on Titus 2:3-5, this study teaches young women about godly character, healthy relationships, and managing a home.

Also available in Portuguese (Seja Surpreendente: Estudo a luz da Biblia para a mulher surpreendente de hoje)

INVINCIBLE LOVE, INVISIBLE WAR

An excellent study for those who want to be prepared for spiritual battles by being armed with God's Word.

THE AMAZING TEMPERAMENTS

This 6-week study biblically explores the strengths and weaknesses of each personality type to reach a full understanding and appreciation of yourself and others.

THE AMAZING LIFE OF JESUS CHRIST, PART ONE AND PART TWO

A chronological study of the Gospels that teaches about Christ's life in a deeper, more intentional way.

EMPOWERED: THE AMAZING CHURCH OF JESUS CHRIST

A study of the Book of Acts highlighting the growth of the church through the power of the Holy Spirit.

WHO IS JESUS?

A short study highlighting the attributes of Jesus, including:

The Resurrection and The Life

READY TO DIG IN?

Scan this QR code using your smartphone to preview our Bible studies and find out more about **Big Dream Ministries**.

23622902R00120